90 Years of the Canaries on Camera

THE
Norwich City
STORY

90 Years of the Canaries on Camera

THE Norwich City STORY

Eastern Daily Press

Breedon Books
Publishing Company
Derby

First published in Great Britain by
The Breedon Books Publishing Company Limited
44 Friar Gate, Derby, DE1 1DA.
1995

ISBN 1 85983 027 7

Printed and bound by Butler & Tanner, Frome, Somerset.
Jacket printed by Premier Print, Nottingham.

Contents

Acknowledgements

This book would not have been possible without the help and support of many people. I would like to thank the photographic department of *Eastern Counties Newspapers* for their prompt attention to my requests for prints, and Steve Snelling for his encouragement throughout the project. I must thank Mike Davage and Dick Middleton for the way their extensive research has made my task easier, and also thank Mike for the loan of several pictures. I am indebted to Ken Nethercott, Bryan Thurlow, Mike Sutton and Ronnie Brooks for their assistance with player identification. Most of all, my debt is to the men who have shaped the history of Norwich City Football Club, and to the reporters and photographers of the *Eastern Daily Press* over many decades who have relayed their achievements to an eager audience.

Photographs

Reproductions of most of the photographs featured in this book can be purchased from Eastern Counties Newspapers, Prospect House, Rouen Road, Norwich.

Introduction

FROM the club's formation in 1902 to the first memorable UEFA Cup campaign of 1993 and the troubled season which followed, the fortunes of Norwich City have captured the imagination of the footballing public of Norfolk and far beyond, and filled thousands upon thousands of column inches in the pages of the *Eastern Daily Press*.

Days of triumph and tragedy, delight and despair, buoyancy and near bankruptcy, celebration and controversy have all been faithfully recorded down the decades by the reporters and photographers of the *EDP*.

Between 1986 and 1992, it was my privilege to travel the length and breadth of England to watch the Canaries in my role as soccer writer for the *EDP* and later, for its sister paper, the *Evening News*.

They were, in the main, years of unparalleled success for City. I saw them finish fifth in Division One in 1987, then better it by finishing fourth two years later. They reached two FA Cup semi-finals, although both were disappointing affairs. Those 1-0 defeats are always the hardest to take.

But throughout that time, I was always conscious of the number of fans who had seen so much more joy and drama and tragedy unfold in their years of following the Canaries. My first day on the terraces at Carrow Road with my father and brother was in 1967, but what of the hundreds, perhaps still a thousand or even more, who remember watching their team at The Nest? There were others who had seen them conquer Liverpool and Arsenal in the FA Cup in those golden years of the early 1950s. And there were thousands, without a

shadow of doubt, who had witnessed the remarkable exploits of Archie Macaulay's team in the FA Cup in 1959. Oh for a time machine to transport us back to White Hart Lane on St Valentine's Day, 1959. There can surely have been no greater sight than City's 20,000 fans streaming into North London and filling the grand old stadium with colour for the fifth-round tie against Tottenham.

Alas, there is no time machine, but from the archives of the *EDP*, we can provide the next best thing with more than 90 years of the Canaries on camera.

I have not endeavoured to write another club history, for the late, great Ted Bell has already done a wonderful job in that respect. But within a chronological framework, I have attempted to recapture the faces and the flavour of some of the most dramatic and significant days in Norwich City history, and reintroduce the men who shaped the destiny of the Canaries.

The 350 pictures I have chosen tell but a fraction of the whole story, but I trust you will enjoy the selection.

As a City fan of some 30 years' standing, I confess their relegation in 1995 – which coincided with the completion of my research for the book – is a cause of some distress. But we have all learned to expect the unexpected from Norwich City down the years. And who is to say we shall not return to battle in Europe in the not too distant future? On the Ball, City!

David Cuffley
Norwich, June 1995

In the Beginning

NORWICH City Football Club can look forward to celebrating their centenary in the year 2002, although earliest records show the existence of a 'Norwich Foot-ball Club' as far back as 1868.

Playing at Newmarket Road and donning colours which might even make the kit designers of the 1990s blush – violet, black, white and yellow – the original club is believed to have survived only four years and followed a code more akin to rugby than association football.

Instead it is to 1902 that one must turn for the opening chapter in the history of Norwich City. The club was formed on Tuesday, 17 June, at a public meeting at the Criterion Café in White Lion Street, Norwich, at the bidding of schoolmasters Robert Webster and Joe Nutchey, until then leading figures with the top club in Norwich, the Church of England Young Men's Society.

City played their first match, a friendly against Harwich, at Newmarket Road on 6 September 1902, and were elected to the Norfolk & Suffolk League.

With Webster as chairman, Nutchey as treasurer and Arthur Turner joint-secretary and the man most responsible for building the side in his bid to make City the top club in East Anglia, they finished third, third and first in their first three seasons in the Norfolk & Suffolk League, and crowds at Newmarket Road swelled to around 6,000.

During City's third season, however, came the bombshell which forced the club into the professional sphere and shaped their entire future. An FA Commission at the Bell Hotel, Norwich, in December 1904, suspended Webster, Nutchey and Turner from football for the rest of the season after City were found guilty of making payments and incurring expenses incompatible with their amateur status.

Having effectively been declared professional, City decided to make it a permanent step. A new chairman was appointed in Wilfrid L.Burgess and on 4 March 1905, the club became officially professional. A limited liability company was formed, a new manager was appointed in John Bowman from Queen's Park Rangers, and on 30 May 1905, City were elected to the Southern League. After only three years of Southern League football, during which time City finished seventh, eighth and 16th, it was clear that a move to a new ground was imperative if the club was to progress up the soccer ladder.

So it was that The Nest, a disused chalk pit in Rosary Road, Norwich, became home to Norwich City for the next 27 years, fashioned into a football stadium in the space of one summer and a daunting sight for visiting teams with a 50ft concrete wall at one end, holding a cliff topped by a row of terraced houses.

Seven more seasons followed before war intervened, but City could finish no higher than tenth in the Southern League.

They had, however, already proved themselves capable of the kind of FA Cup shock which characterised later years in club history.

In their final season at Newmarket Road, they knocked out holders Sheffield Wednesday, and in February 1909 they beat Liverpool 3-2 at Anfield. Sunderland were also a major scalp, beaten 3-1 at The Nest in January 1911.

Norwich City's first professional side face the camera, at a time when they wore blue and white halves and were still known as the 'Citizens'. The season is 1905-06, and City had just taken their place in the Southern League. Back row (left to right): Arthur Archer, James McEwen, Billy Bushell, reserve goalkeeper Warnes. Second row: Charlie Miles (trainer), John Bowman (manager), Bill Childs, Bill Cummings, Charlie Williams, Fred Rose, Fred Bemment, Hugh McQueen (assistant trainer). Third row: Robert Muir, Samuel Graham, Freddy Wilkinson, Duncan Ronaldson, Davie Ross, Horace Brindley, William Linward. Front row: Herbert Vigar, Archie Livingstone.

Controversy over the sale of City's star goalscorers is not a new phenomenon. If the departures of Ron Davies, Hugh Curran, Kevin Reeves and Chris Sutton have all caused an outcry in modern times, there was similar indignation at the transfer of Davie Ross to Manchester City in February 1907 for a Southern League record fee of £650. He scored 49 goals in only 71 matches for City in less than two full seasons, so the uproar was understandable.

Among the earliest surviving action pictures of Norwich City are those which come from their Southern League game at Portsmouth on 14 September 1907. The game finished in a 1-1 draw and here City goalkeeper Fred Thompson is pictured punching clear during a Portsmouth attack. The Norwich team sheet that day read: Thompson, Newlands, McEwen, Hutchinson, Bushell, Livingstone, Muir, Young, Bauchop, Smith, Allsopp.

More action from Portsmouth v Norwich City in the Southern League on 14 September 1907. Pompey's James Thompson is seen here scoring a penalty in the 1-1 draw at Fratton Park. Norwich's goal came from James Young, a Scottish inside-right who joined the club from Bristol Rovers. City had in fact beaten Portsmouth 4-0 at home 12 days earlier, in the first match of the season. But Portsmouth finished the season ninth in the table, with City 16th, only four places off the bottom.

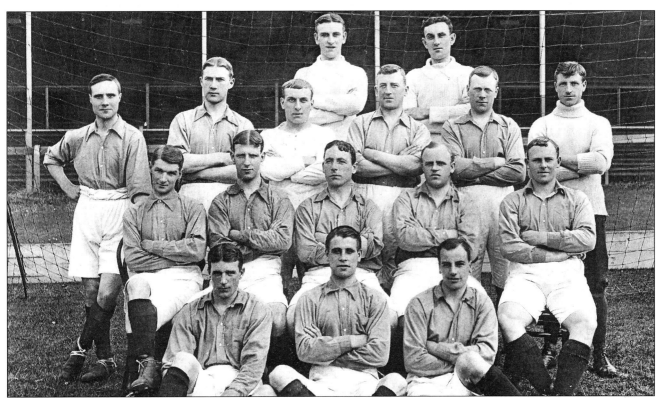

This was how Norwich City lined up in 1907-08, their last season at Newmarket Road before moving to The Nest. It was largely a season of struggle in the Southern League, City finishing 16th. But these players were responsible for the club's first glorious giantkilling feat. FA Cup holders Sheffield Wednesday were the visitors for a first-round tie on 11 January 1908. Wednesday had beaten Everton 2-1 in the 1907 Final, but went down 2-0 to Norwich in frosty conditions at Newmarket Road in front of 10,366 fans as their defence of the trophy came to an abrupt end. Ten of the side who beat Wednesday are pictured on this team group, including goalscorers Jimmy Bauchop and Tommy Allsopp. Back row: Peter Roney, Fred Thompson. Second row: Billy Bushell, Albert Jones, Bobby Whiteman, Archie Livingstone, Gerry Newlands, Hugh McQueen (assistant trainer). Third row: Robert Muir, George Lamberton, James McEwen, Wally Smith, Tommy Allsopp. Front row: James Young, Jimmy Bauchop, Harry Hutchinson.

Norwich City's staff pictured in 1908. Back row (left to right): A.Turner (assistant manager), J.C.Nutchey (referee), J.W.Howes (honorary secretary and director), J.Pyke (chairman), M.Nattrass (director), A.E.Barnham (director), W.T.Blyth (director). Second row: Newlands, Long, G.Martin, C.Greenfield, Tomlinson, Wagstaff, G.Porter, Roney, Beale, McQueen (trainer). Seated: Livingstone, Coxhead, McEwen (captain), Flanagan, Whiteman, Allsopp. On ground: Church, Smith, Silor, Pegg.

The modern term 'midfielder' was unheard of when John William Chick formed an important part of City's half-back line before World War One. Chick made 49 appearances for Norwich between 1909 and 1911, playing at left-half, before moving on to Rochdale. He was a member of the City side who beat Crystal Palace at The Nest in October 1909 in front of a crowd of 12,078, then a ground record.

Stiff formality and perfect symmetry were the order of the day when the City team of 1909-10 lined up at The Nest for this team picture. But among the well-dressed gentlemen mingling with the 22 players are two of the best-known faces from the formative years in club history. Standing on the extreme left of the second row, wearing flat cap and waistcoat, is Charlie Miles, appointed trainer in 1905 by manager John Bowman. And seated third from the left on the front row is Arthur Turner pictured in what proved to be his first and last season as team manager. Turner, appointed joint secretary when the club was formed in 1902, was shown the door in March 1910, the end of his long association with City. He was replaced by James Stansfield and Norwich finished sixth from bottom of the Southern League.

Left: Among the earliest pairs of brothers to sign for City were Harold and Reg Levi, on 30 August 1910. Younger brother Harold made 22 appearances for Norwich in the Southern League in season 1910-11, playing at outside-left, before moving on to Queen's Park Rangers. Reg failed to make the City first team and moved on to Oldham Athletic, but he was a capable long-distance runner, winning the Windsor to London Marathon. Both brothers died relatively young, Harold at Hendon on 4 October 1941 at the age of 49, and Reg at Willesden on 22 May 1946, aged 57.

George 'Pompey' Martin must have appeared on more City team pictures than most after a career which spanned 14 years at The Nest. Signed from Portsmouth in 1913 – hence the nickname – he went on to make a total of 337 first-team appearances for City, the last of them in 1927, most of them at centre-half. His one and only goal in all that time came in a 6-3 home win over Bournemouth in October, 1924. 'Pompey' had two testimonials during his time with the club and died in Norwich in 1962.

City finished seventh from bottom of the Southern League in 1913-14, the last full season before the outbreak of World War One. They picked up points steadily for two-thirds of the season, but won only two of their last 13 League matches. Pictured here are (left to right): Back row: George Bell, George MacDonald. Second row: Cecil Potter, Harry Woods, Arthur Wolstenholme, James Kennedy. Third row: Billy Hampson, Jack Houghton, Billy Ingham, Ben Smith, Joe Lansdale, William Mellor, John Allen, Frank Hill, Wally Taylor, Arthur Woodland. Front row: James B.Stansfield (manager), George Martin, Percy Sutcliffe, Thomas Valentine, Charles Curtin, Alfred Boland, George Ritchie, Danny Wilson, Jock Mackenzie, Charlie Miles (trainer).

Between the Wars

DEBTS of some £3,000 incurred by Norwich City during World War One forced the club to be wound up in December 1917, but a new company was formed in February 1919 and six months later, City were back in action in the Southern League.

It was but a brief reintroduction to non-League football, for in May 1920 the Football League agreed to accept the Southern League First Division clubs' proposition that a new Third Division be formed.

As a result, City kicked off their Football League career in August 1920 just as they had done on their Southern League baptism 15 years earlier, with an away match at Plymouth, where they earned a 1-1 draw.

Norwich finished their first Football League season 16th in Division Three, a modest performance but one which was to set the tone for the 1920s, when their highest position was 11th in 1923-24.

The arrival of Jimmy Kerr as manager in 1929 saw City climb to a best-ever eighth place in May 1930, but in a perverse twist to be repeated several times in the decades ahead, they managed to undo much of the good work by finishing bottom 12 months later!

It was not until the 1932-33 season that the Canaries turned the corner, mounting a sustained promotion challenge until three defeats in April forced them to settle for third place. Manager Kerr died in February 1933, but had already laid the foundations for what proved to be a memorable season for City in 1933-34.

With former Southampton and Arsenal full-back Tom Parker at the helm as manager, the Canaries stormed to the Division Three South championship by a margin of seven points.

Their new-found Second Division status brought its own problems, though, and while City achieved a respectable 14th place in their first season in more exalted company, it proved to be their final campaign at The Nest.

Doubtless prompted by a record crowd of 25,037 in the stadium for the FA Cup visit of Sheffield Wednesday in February 1935, the FA decreed that The Nest was unsafe for big attendances and, in what was described as a two-month building miracle, City's new home at Carrow Road was built from scratch during the close season and opened on time on 31 August 1935, when West Ham were the visitors.

The Canaries enjoyed four more seasons of Second Division football at their new ground before the outbreak of war – or at least they enjoyed the first three, for 1938-39 saw them return from whence they came, relegated on goal-average after finishing second from bottom of the division.

Back to square one, possibly not, but it was to be more than 20 years before the Canaries regained Second Division status.

Inside-left Arthur 'Tricky' Hawes was one of the earliest City exports to make his name with a bigger club. Born at Swanton Morley, he joined the club at the age of 19 a year after the outbreak of World War One, and when Southern League action resumed in 1919-20, he scored eight times in 37 matches before moving to South Shields. Sunderland snapped him up for £1,750 in 1921 and he spent nearly six years at Roker Park, during which time the North-East club finished in the top three in Division One four times. Hawes returned to Norwich at the end of his career.

City re-formed in 1919 after World War One and for what proved to be their final season in the Southern League, 1919-20, they were managed by Major Frank Buckley. City finished 12th in a modest season, but behind the scenes there was constant discord and Major Buckley resigned at the end of the season. He went on to a varied managerial career, most successfully with Wolves, who were runners-up in both the championship and FA Cup under his guidance in 1939.

Left: One of a long line of Norwich-born players and one-club men to don City colours was Ben Smith, a full-back who made the transition from Southern League to Football League with the club. He was one of 40 players, a remarkable tally, used in the 1919-20 season by City, their last before becoming part of the Football League. Smith died in Norwich in 1972, aged 79.

Right: George Addy was one of a select band in City history – as one of the 11 who played in the club's first-ever Football League game at Plymouth on 28 August 1920. Barnsley-born and primarily a left-half, he made 33 first-team appearances for Norwich, scoring six times. He played football for the Royal Welch Fusiliers during World War One.

Left: Half-back Reg Wilkinson was another of those who played in City's first-ever Football League match against Plymouth, and he made 113 appearances in all for the club. Norwich-born, he had a distinguished Army football career and joined City in 1919. His move to Sunderland in 1923 proved brief and unsuccessful, but a year later he joined Brighton and stayed for ten years, making nearly 400 appearances for the South Coast club. He was only 47 when he collapsed and died playing for Norwich Electricity.

Right: Herbert Skermer had the honour of being the goalkeeper in City's first-ever Football League game at Plymouth in 1920 and was one of only two ever-presents in the 1920-21 season, the other being right-back George Gray. In all, Skermer made 95 first-team appearances for City, the first of them in 1919 in the club's last season in the Southern League. He later became licensee of a pub called the Lame Dog in Norwich.

Joe Hannah was a local hero in every sense of the word. Born at Sheringham, he joined City in August 1920, made his first-team debut at Newport in January 1921 and went on to make 427 senior appearances over the next 14 years, mostly at right-half or right-back. His City career lasted just long enough for him to play in more than half the Division Three South programme of 1933-34, when they won the championship. A knee injury sustained against Torquay in a Division Three South Cup semi-final effectively ended his career at the age of 35. But only Kevin Keelan, Ron Ashman and Dave Stringer played more senior games for the club, and few players of the modern era are likely to pass that total.

Bob Dennison scored City's first-ever home Football League goal, ending an extraordinarily barren run at The Nest. Norwich failed to score in their first five home games of 1920-21, but Dennison struck in a 1-1 draw with Bristol Rovers on 30 October 1920, a week after scoring twice in the corresponding away fixture. In all, he bagged a healthy 38 goals in 126 senior games for City before joining Brighton. When his League career ended, he came back to Norfolk and played for a year for Yarmouth Town.

The 1922-23 season was not a memorable one for City. They finished fifth from bottom in Division Three South and were knocked out of the FA Cup at The Nest in the first round by Bolton Wanderers, who won 2-0 on their way to winning the trophy in the first Wembley Final. The only consolation for City was a gate of 15,286 at The Nest in trying financial times. One familiar face on this team picture made his first appearance during that season – goalkeeper Charlie Dennington, sixth from the left on the back row, who was born at Beccles and went on to make 209 first-team appearances for City up to 1929. He was the first goalkeeper to play 100 League games for the club.

Those distinctive yellow and green shirts have not been a permanent feature of City's strip. The club started life playing in blue and white halves, and for a brief spell from 1923 to 1925, the Canaries wore white shirts. This team picture was taken before the start of the 1924-25 season, a moderate one, in which City finished 12th in Division Three South.

Left: More than 300 footballers have played for England only once – and Sam Austin was one of them, lining up against the Irish in 1925. But before that, the outside-right spent nearly four years with Norwich, scoring 39 goals in 164 appearances and moving to Manchester City in 1924 for £2,000. He played for Manchester City in the 1926 FA Cup Final, but they were beaten 1-0 by Bolton Wanderers.

Right: Percy Varco was one of the true legends of Norwich City history, despite a relatively brief spell of two and a half years with the club. Born at Fowey in Cornwall, he joined City in the summer of 1927 after spells with Torquay, Aston Villa and Queen's Park Rangers. Centre-forward Varco scored ten goals in his first seven League games for Norwich and by the time he played his last match for the club at Queen's Park Rangers on Boxing Day, 1929, he had 47 goals in 65 senior appearances, an exceptional strike rate. A week later, he joined Exeter on a free transfer!

The most famous sportsman of all on this Norwich City team picture from late 1931 never made a first-team appearance for the club. But Bill Edrich (front row, extreme right), later to become one of England's all-time cricketing greats, was with City as an amateur up to 1934, before moving to Tottenham, for whom he made 20 first-team appearances, scoring four goals. Edrich the cricketer went on to play 39 Tests and captained both Middlesex and Norfolk. This team picture was taken at King's Lynn, where City played a friendly as part of the deal which brought Bernard Robinson to The Nest. Back row (left to right): Bob Young, Jimmy Kerr (manager), Joe Hannah, Doug Lochhead, Bernard Robinson, Tom Williamson, Robert Robinson, Cecil Blakemore, R.G.Pilch snr. Front row: Bill 'Ginger' Smith, Frank Pegg, Stan Ramsay, Tommy Hunt, Bill Edrich.

Some idea of the cramped conditions at The Nest can be gleaned from this action shot, which appears to come from the early 1930s, though the exact date and the identity of opponents are uncertain. In this untidy goalmouth scramble, the visitors are claiming a goal, while the City defender on the line seems ready to mount his own protest. At least the referee is well positioned to judge, long before television action replays were around to prove him wrong!

This is how the Canaries lined up in the 1932-33 season, when they finished third in Division Three South. In late March 1933, they topped the table, but three successive defeats in April cost them dear and they slipped to third behind Brentford and Exeter. It all came right a year later, however, when City lifted the championship. Back row (left to right): Bernard Robinson, Joe Hannah, Robert Robinson, Bob Young (trainer), Stan Ramsay, Doug Lochhead. Front row: Ken Burditt, Tom Scott, Tom Williamson, Oliver Brown, Cec Blakemore, Lionel Murphy.

Jack Vinall's tally of 80 goals for the Canaries has been bettered only by Johnny Gavin and Terry Allcock, and two of those goals came in the first match at Carrow Road against West Ham in 1935, giving him a special place in club history. Vinall joined the club in the summer of 1933, a key signing by Tom Parker as City swept all before them on their way to the Division Three South championship. The Birmingham-born centre-forward eventually moved to Luton for £3,000 in October 1937, proof that selling their best goalscorers is by no means a recent trend with City.

A crowd of 13,219 turned up at The Nest to celebrate City's Division Three South championship success on Monday, 7 May 1934. Second Division champions Grimsby Town were the visitors for the Norfolk & Norwich Hospital Cup match, which raised £680 for the charity. City gave a performance which befitted the occasion, winning 7-2 with five goals from Jack Vinall and two from Alf Kirchen. The two teams are pictured before kick-off with their respective divisional shields, and in the centre, the Hospital Cup.

City's days at The Nest were numbered because of fears over safety when crowds such as this packed into the ground. 16 February 1935, brought Sheffield Wednesday to Norwich for an FA Cup fifth-round tie and they attracted a record crowd of 25,037 to The Nest. England outside-left Ellis Rimmer scored the only goal as Wednesday kept on course for the Final, where they beat West Bromwich Albion 4-2 at Wembley, Rimmer scoring twice. In May the FA warned City that The Nest may no longer be suitable for big crowds, and by the end of August they had moved to the newly-built Carrow Road stadium.

Left: Alf Kirchen's City career was brief and spectacular before a £6,000 move took him to Arsenal in March 1935. The flying right winger, born at Shouldham in Norfolk, joined the Canaries in 1933 and made his first-team debut in the penultimate match of the Division Three South championship campaign. The following season, he scored ten goals in only 17 appearances, enough to earn his passage to Highbury, where he won a championship medal and England caps against Norway, Sweden and Finland. Wartime took his prime years and an ankle injury ended his career before the war was over. He was a City director during the 1950s.

Right: Billy Furness made his name as an inside-left with Leeds United in the early 1930s and was capped by England against Italy in May 1933. Norwich City snapped him up for £2,750 in June 1937 and he played for the Canaries before and after the war, scoring 21 times in 96 senior matches before retiring in 1947. He later served the club as trainer and physiotherapist. He died in Norwich in 1980 at the age of 71.

The first £1 million arrival at Carrow Road was more than half a century away – and it might have been light years away – when the Canaries made their last signing before World War Two. Left-back John Milburn, not surprisingly known as Jack, arrived from Leeds United for the princely sum of £2,000 on 24 February, 1939. He is pictured being welcomed to Norwich by Bob Young. Milburn played the last 15 matches of season 1938-39, but there was to be no happy ending. City were relegated from Division Two on goal-average – and Milburn missed a penalty in the penultimate match, a 1-0 defeat at Plymouth.

Post-war Rise and Fall

BETWEEN the time Football League action resumed at Carrow Road in 1946 and the day when the Canaries stood on the brink of bankruptcy nearly 11 years later, the mood of supporters must have swung wildly between delight and despair at the exploits of their beloved team.

The club faced an uphill battle from the word go when peacetime soccer got under way, heavily in debt and desperately short of established players.

Yet despite two seasons of struggle which resulted in having to seek re-election in both 1947 and 1948, support for City was remarkably strong and the faith of the fans was rewarded by a gradual improvement in results under the management of Doug Lochhead and, more especially, Norman Low.

Low, player-manager for half a season before his appointment was confirmed in May 1950, led City through a five-year spell of great success in Division Three South.

The Canaries finished second, third and fourth in his first three seasons in charge, and in 1950-51 they were desperately unlucky to miss out on promotion.

Beaten only seven times in 46 matches, they chalked up 64 points, more than the champions of the division for the previous three seasons. But on this occasion, Nottingham Forest had an even more remarkable campaign, amassing 70.

With only one team promoted, City missed out, and when they finished a modest 12th in 1955, Low was shown the door with what proved to be disastrous consequences.

His reign had also been marked by more FA Cup giant-killing exploits as two-goal Tom Docherty inspired the Canaries to a 3-1 third-round victory over Liverpool at Carrow Road in January 1951, and two goals from Tom Johnston set up a thrilling 2-1 win over Arsenal at Highbury in the fourth round in 1954.

But such glorious days must have seemed little more than faded memories as City plunged headlong into crisis less than two years after Low's departure.

Tom Parker, who had guided City to championship success in 1934, was recalled as manager in 1955, and inspired by 31 League goals from star signing Ralph Hunt, the Canaries rose to seventh in 1955-56. But the following season was a disaster for City, who at one stage went 25 League games without a win, and as gates dropped below 10,000, were on the brink of financial ruin.

The Norfolk News Company, publishers of the Eastern Daily Press, paid one week's £500 wage bill before a public appeal led by the Lord Mayor of Norwich, Arthur South, raised more than £20,000 to rescue the club. At the same time, there was a new board elected under Geoffrey Watling and a new manager recruited in Archie Macaulay. Need one say more?

The Canaries finished second from bottom in Division Three South in the first two seasons after the war, and midway through the 1947-48 campaign, they changed manager. Cyril Spiers was replaced by Doug Lochhead, who had already given the club such sterling service as player, assistant manager and interim manager in the immediate post-war period. And in spite of their poor results, support for the Canaries was exceptional. In 1947-48 attendances averaged more than 20,000 for the first time. Back row (left to right): Bert Holmes, Bernard Robinson, Allenby Driver, Norman Low, Ken Nethercott, Don Edwards, Derek Davis, Grenville Williams, Jimmy Guy, Leslie Dawes, Maurice Tobin. Second row: Billy Furness (assistant trainer), Fred Mansfield, Denis Morgan, Trevor Rowlands, Oscar Hold, Albert Foan, Johnny Church, Ivan Armes, Eric Arnold, Leslie Eyre, Fred Hall ('A' team trainer). Front row: Don Pickwick, Len Dutton, Noel Kinsey, Harry Proctor (trainer), Doug Lochhead (manager) Peter Dash (secretary), Terry Ryder, Sid Jones, George Morgan. Seated in front: Maldwyn Rees, Denys Jones.

Bernard Robinson's City career stretched from 1931 to 1949, a remarkable length of service for one of the club's all-time most popular players. But for the war, he might well have passed the 600 mark in appearances. As it was, his total of 380 first-team matches put him in the top ten in club history. Born at Cambridge in 1911, he joined Norwich from King's Lynn as a 19-year-old and was a member of the team which won the Division Three South championship in 1934. A right-half, he played 160 wartime games and finished his career playing at right-back. His last senior match was, fittingly, a 2-0 local derby victory over Ipswich in March 1949.

With 69 goals in 201 appearances, Leslie Eyre was one of the most consistent goalscorers in City's history – and never more deadly than on 30 November 1946, when he scored five times at Carrow Road in a 7-2 FA Cup win over Brighton. Still sixth in the club's all-time goalscoring list, he was also on target in the memorable 3-1 FA Cup victory over Liverpool in January 1951. It was in that 1950-51 season that the Canaries finished second to Nottingham Forest in Division Three South, but missed out on promotion at a time when only one team went up, and it is from that season that this picture comes, taken on 23 August 1950, during a goalless draw against Northampton at Carrow Road. Leslie Eyre died in 1991 at the age of 69.

Few players have made a more dramatic start to their Norwich City career than centre-forward Roy Hollis, who scored a hat-trick on his senior debut in a 5-2 home win over Queen's Park Rangers in April, 1948. It was a sign of things to come as he chalked up 59 goals in 107 first-team appearances for the Canaries, including five in an 8-0 win over Walsall in 1951, before moving to Tottenham in 1952. It was at Southend, however, that he spent the longest spell of his career, and his 122 goals for the Essex club included a hat-trick against City in a Christmas fixture in 1954 – making him the only man to score three times for and against Norwich in a match at Carrow Road. Born at Great Yarmouth, Hollis played for his home-town club before and after his Football League career.

Don Pickwick was part of a formidable half-back line fielded by the Canaries in the early 1950s, completed by two more great club servants in Reg Foulkes and Ron Ashman. Pickwick joined City in February 1946 and spent ten years with the club before moving to Spalding United as player-manager. A Welsh schoolboy international – but at Rugby Union – he made a total of 244 first-team appearances for City, and such was his commitment to the Canary cause that he played for them on his wedding day in a 1-1 draw at Colchester!

The Canaries paid a club record fee of £9,500 for Alf Ackerman when he joined them from Hull City in August 1951. A South African, he scored a tidy 35 goals in only 70 senior matches for the club before returning to Hull in October 1953. In his two full seasons with City, they finished third and fourth in Division Three South. In his first season at Carrow Road, Norwich doubled Ipswich and Ackerman scored in both matches. Not until 1995 did they again complete a League double over Town. In later life, he returned to South Africa to live and died in Transvaal in 1988 at the age of 59.

John Duffy spent much of his five-year spell with the Canaries battling with Denis Morgan for the right-back spot, but in 1950-51 he was a virtual fixture at No 2 as City finished second in Division Three South and knocked Liverpool out of the FA Cup at Carrow Road. A Glaswegian who joined Norwich from Clyde in 1949, he went on to play for Yarmouth Town for four seasons.

Much-travelled centre-forward Tom Johnston enjoyed a fruitful spell with the Canaries from 1952 to 1954, scoring 33 times in only 67 first-team matches. It was a strike rate he maintained after moving to Newport County, and later Leyton Orient, Blackburn and Gillingham. Johnston, who scored both goals in City's FA Cup win at Arsenal in 1954, was the only player to score four goals in an away League match for City before Efan Ekoku repeated the feat at Everton in 1993. From a mining background, he always played with his left wrist bandaged to protect an injury from his days in the pits. In his entire Football League career, he scored 237 goals.

If you thought the Canaries' UEFA Cup-tie against Vitesse Arnhem in 1993 broke new ground, they in fact went Dutch more than 40 years before that – though it is fairly certain they did not take the field in this particular strip. The picture was taken at Volendam on 21 May 1952, during City's four-match tour of Holland. The same line-up took on a Hague Combined XI later the same day, winning 2-1. Front row (left to right): Harry Proctor (trainer), Ron Ashman, Johnny Gavin, Denis Morgan, Reg Foulkes, Noel Kinsey, Len Dutton and Norman Low (manager). Front row: Bill Lewis, Don Pickwick, Ken Nethercott, Roy Hollis and John Summers.

The face is instantly recognisable to anyone who watched the Canaries in the '50s – that of Johnny Gavin, the leading goalscorer in the club's history with 132 goals. A £1,500 capture from Limerick, right winger Gavin's City career was split into two spells, punctuated by a year with Tottenham in which he scored a healthy 15 goals in 32 League matches. Attending a players' reunion in 1990, he was still proud of his place at the top of the scoring charts for Norwich. A Republic of Ireland international with seven caps between 1950 and 1957, Gavin was with City from 1948 to 1954, when he moved to White Hart Lane, returning to Carrow Road a year later as part of the deal which took centre-half Maurice Norman to Spurs.

One of the Canaries' most remarkable FA Cup triumphs of all came at Highbury in the fourth round on 30 January 1954, when they beat mighty Arsenal 2-1 in front of a crowd of 55,767. It was a victory achieved in difficult circumstances, with Bobby Brennan missing a penalty and being sent off along with Arsenal's Alex Forbes. But two second-half goals from Tom Johnston were enough to clinch a famous win. Here City's Roy McCrohan challenges Arsenal's Don Roper in the air, while Lionel Smith (3) looks on.

The Canaries received a heroes' welcome on arriving back at Norwich after their FA Cup victory at Arsenal in 1954. Manager Norman Low is pictured (centre, second from front) with Ron Ashman and Bill Lewis on either side. Behind Low, Bobby Brennan holds his child up to the camera, with goalkeeper Ken Oxford next to them. Roy McCrohan, behind them, waves his left hand in celebration, while the wavy-haired Reg Foulkes is on the right of the picture, halfway back, with Peter Gordon in front of him (partially obscured by flat cap).

The financial crisis which almost forced City out of business in 1956-57 led to the formation of a new board of directors, elected at an Extraordinary General Meeting of shareholders at Samson and Hercules House on Monday, 4 February 1957. A lengthy ballot went on until nearly 1am and four of the five directors chosen are pictured here (from left to right): Frederick Jex, James Hanly, George Fish and Geoffrey Watling, the new chairman. Fish became vice-chairman. The fifth director, Henry Robinson, was not at the meeting. Second from the right is Arthur South, then Lord Mayor of Norwich, who chaired the meeting.

City centre-forward Ralph Hunt hammered 72 goals in only 132 League and Cup appearances for the club, between 1955 and 1958, and stands fourth in the Canaries' all-time goalscoring charts. He was able to maintain that phenomenal strike rate at each of his subsequent clubs – Derby, Grimsby, Swindon, Port Vale, Newport and Chesterfield. Hunt joined City from Bournemouth in July 1955 and scored 33 times in his first season with the club. He had a career total of 186 goals in 374 League games when, at the age of 31, he died in Grantham & Kesteven Hospital from injuries sustained in a car crash, in December 1964.

Arthur South – later Sir Arthur – played the lead role in steering Norwich City away from extinction in 1956-57, and went on to serve the Canaries as a tireless chairman from 1973 to 1985. As Lord Mayor of Norwich, he chaired the Appeal Fund which was launched in December 1956 with the aim of raising £25,000 to keep the club in business. He is pictured here addressing shareholders at the extraordinary general meeting on 4 February 1957. Ted Bell wrote in *On The Ball, City* that 'the meeting itself was controlled by Mr South with the adroitness and skill of an elder statesman'.

It was decided that a board of up to 12 directors was too unwieldy and the advisory committee recommended that between four and six was a more suitable number. As it was, five directors were appointed at the extraordinary general meeting, among them former chairman James Hanly. The ballot went on until nearly 1am, with shareholders shown here considering their votes.

City shareholders arrive at the Samson and Hercules House for an historic night in club history. Not everyone was entirely happy, however, with events in the build-up to the meeting. Len Votier, president of the City Supporters' Club and a member of the Appeal Committee, withdrew his nomination as a candidate for the board because he claimed the election was 'cut and dried' before the meeting even took place. He was also upset at the suggestion that the Supporters' Club could have contributed more to the struggling football club.

Elected chairman of Norwich City at the crisis meeting of February 1957, Geoffrey Watling became the guiding hand behind the club through some of its finest days – the FA Cup run of 1959 and promotion to Division Two the following year, the Second Division championship season of 1971-72 and a first Wembley appearance a year later. He resigned after 16 years as chairman, the longest serving in club history, in 1973. But the prominent Norwich businessman remains as devoted a follower of the Canaries' fortunes as ever in his role as club president, pictured here in 1986. After City had gained promotion in 1972, Ted Bell wrote of Mr Watling in his book, *On The Ball, City*: 'The man with the biggest smile must have been Geoffrey Watling. Criticised at times to the point where he must have wondered whether it was worth the effort, he remained unswerving in his devotion to the club.'

1959 and All That

IF ONE period in Norwich City's history has captured the imagination of the soccer public more than any other – more even than their first European adventure in 1993 – it has to be ten magical weeks in early 1959.

Mention that year to any supporter who witnessed the exploits of Archie Macaulay's Third Division giantkillers in that most magical of competitions, the FA Cup, and his or her eyes are likely to light up, followed by the almost automatic reeling off of the names of a team which shook the football world.

Manchester United, Cardiff City, Tottenham Hotspur and Sheffield United were the main victims of a Canary success story which took them to the brink of a Wembley Final before the heartbreak of semi-final defeat at the hands of moderate Luton Town.

The most cynical observer was won over by the way Macaulay's team disposed of supposedly higher class opposition not with a robust style associated with the lower divisions, but by beating them at their own game – outplayed and out-thought as well as outfought.

After victories over Ilford and Swindon Town in the opening two rounds, it was a 3-0 win over Manchester United at icy Carrow Road in round three which triggered City's amazing run and galvanised the fans into a frenzy of FA Cup excitement that was to last for more than two months.

They scraped together every available penny for trips to White Hart Lane, Bramall Lane and St Andrew's. They dressed in the most extraordinary costumes to display their allegiance to a team now treated more like film stars than footballers. And when it was all over, they welcomed their team home like conquering heroes.

Today, players such as Ron Ashman, Ken Nethercott, Terry Bly and Bryan Thurlow recall their exploits with modesty, almost embarrassment and some degree of astonishment that so much fuss is still made about the boys of '59.

But for those who shared the experience from terrace and stand, the images are powerful and here is another chance to relive one of the most exciting periods in club history.

One of the best signings Norwich City ever made came on 12 March 1958, when they snapped up Terry Allcock from Bolton Wanderers. Over the next 11 years he made a total of 389 first-team appearances for the club, scoring 127 goals, making him second in the Canaries' all-time goalscoring charts. Allcock was a key figure in the side which reached the FA Cup semi-finals in 1959 and won promotion to Division Two the following year. When his playing days were over, he worked as first-team coach under Ron Saunders as City won the Second Division championship in 1972 and reached Wembley for the first time in the 1973 League Cup Final. Allcock is pictured signing for City, watched by club chairman Geoffrey Watling (left) and manager Archie Macaulay.

Former Scottish international Archie Macaulay was the man behind City's tremendous resurgence in the late 1950s. Capped seven times by his country at wing-half, he took over as manager at Carrow Road in April 1957, recruited from Dundee, where he was trainer-coach. Regarded as one of the best coaches and tacticians in the game, he steered City into eighth place in Division Three South in his first season in charge, enough to earn them a place in the new Division Three, and the next two seasons were the most exciting yet in the club's history as the Canaries reached the FA Cup semi-finals and, in 1959-60, gained promotion to Division Two. Among his signings were Terry Allcock, Barry Butler, Jimmy Hill, Errol Crossan and Matt Crowe. City even finished fourth in Division Two in 1960-61, the first season after promotion, but in October 1961, Macaulay resigned to take over at West Bromwich Albion – a sad and sudden end to a glorious four and a half years in charge.

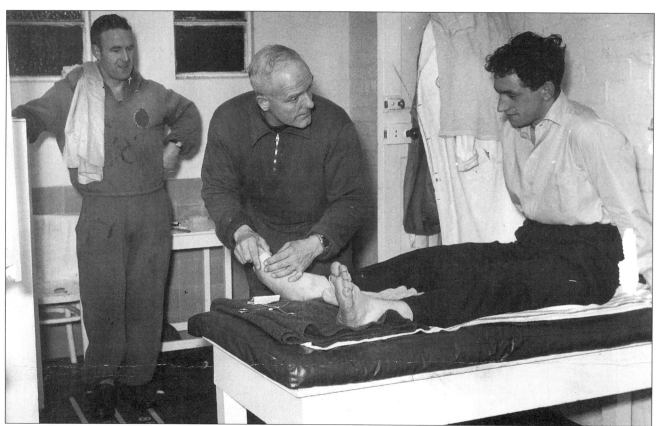

Trainer Harry Topping was manager Archie Macaulay's right-hand man during the FA Cup campaign of 1958-59 and in the promotion campaign which followed. He arrived at Carrow Road from Aldershot after a spell in Holland. Ted Bell said of Topping in his book, *Canary Crusade*, that he was 'a man who stands no nonsense – and his voice from the trainer's bench on match days is proof enough of how much he is wrapped up in the fortunes of the Canaries'. Topping (centre) is pictured in the treatment room, with Jimmy Moran on the table and Harry Proctor looking on.

After disposing of Ilford and Swindon Town in the first two rounds, City's giantkilling crusade began with a stunning 3-0 success over Manchester United at Carrow Road on 10 January 1959. Terry Bly (extreme left) scores the opening goal after 31 minutes from a cross from Bobby Brennan, just visible through the netting, to set the Canaries on their way to victory. The challenge from United's Joe Carolan (3) is too late.

The pressure's on Manchester United as goalkeeper Harry Gregg prepares to meet a cross with City centre-forward Terry Bly waiting to pounce and defender Bill Foulkes behind this pair. Bly scored twice in the Canaries' 3-0 victory.

Anxious times on the Manchester United bench for Matt Busby as his side suffer a shock exit at the hands of the Canaries. United had reached the Final the previous two seasons, losing to Aston Villa in 1957 and Bolton in 1958, their team substantially rebuilt between those two Wembley appearances because of the Munich disaster.

All for one and one for all as City defend in numbers during a rare Manchester United attack in the third round at Carrow Road. The Canaries (left to right) in a snowbound goalmouth are Ken Nethercott, Bryan Thurlow, Ron Ashman, Barry Butler, Roy McCrohan, Matt Crowe (6) and Jimmy Hill.

The City team who beat Manchester United in the third round and went on to make the headlines for the first three months of 1959. Back row (left to right): Roy McCrohan, Bryan Thurlow, Ken Nethercott, Barry Butler, Ron Ashman, Matt Crowe. Front row: Errol Crossan, Terry Allcock, Terry Bly, Jimmy Hill, Bobby Brennan.

No player has donned the Canary yellow shirt with more pride and distinction than Ron Ashman, seen here after one of his side's FA Cup triumphs of 1959. His playing career with City spanned 16 years and he served as acting manager, then manager from December 1962 to June 1966. His total of 662 appearances for the first team has been beaten only by Kevin Keelan, the goalkeeper he signed in July 1963. His career tally of 56 goals for the Canaries stems from the fact that he started out at centre-forward before reverting to half-back for much of the 1950s and finally to left-back in his last few memorable seasons with the club. Ashman suffered a hard time from the fans at Carrow Road in his early years but won them over to such an extent that few men have inspired such affection among City followers. Interviewed last year, when he returned to Carrow Road to meet some of his old colleagues, he said: "I never regretted spending my career there. I would do it all again."

Left: Roy McCrohan began City's FA Cup campaign playing at right-back, but switched to right-half as part of manager Macaulay's tactical reshuffle and made the number-four shirt his own until 1962, when he moved to Colchester. An extensive coaching career eventually took him to the United States in the late 1970s, but before that, he spent five years with Luton Town, becoming assistant manager, an ironic twist after the Hatters broke City hearts in 1959!

Right: Matt Crowe was one of the heroes of the City side which reached the FA Cup semi-final, and a permanent fixture at left-half for the next two seasons. It's astonishing now to think that the Canaries paid only £500 to sign him from Partick Thistle in 1957! He made a total of 214 appearances for City, scoring 18 goals, moving to Brentford in 1962.

A crowd of 67,633 squeezed into White Hart Lane on 14 February 1959, including an estimated 20,000 City fans, for the fifth-round match against Tottenham. Here, Spurs goalkeeper John Hollowbread comes under pressure from Terry Allcock following a City corner. Peter Baker is the Tottenham right-back, with Terry Bly the other Norwich forward and Errol Crossan watching from the flank.

Tottenham on the attack against the Canaries at White Hart Lane as future England centre-forward Bobby Smith lets fly from the edge of the area. But goalkeeper Ken Nethercott was equal to this effort, and City kept Spurs out until a last-ditch equaliser forced a Carrow Road replay.

City full-back Bryan Thurlow in hot pursuit of Tottenham's Dave Dunmore during the FA Cup fifth-round clash at White Hart Lane. Loddon-born Thurlow and centre-forward Terry Bly were the two local lads in the giantkilling City side. Thurlow went on to make a total of 224 senior appearances for the Canaries and was part of an FA touring party which travelled to New Zealand and the Far East in 1961, a squad which also included Bobby Moore and the great Tom Finney as player-manager.

The agony and the ecstasy of it all, perfectly captured on this picture, taken in the final minute of City's FA Cup fifth-round match at Tottenham on St Valentine's Day, 1959. Contrast the celebrations of the Spurs players, including Bobby Smith (9), after Cliff Jones has equalised, with the disbelief of the Canaries. Goalkeeper Nethercott and skipper Ashman are on the floor, while Butler (5), Allcock and McCrohan (4) stand speechless. There was no reprieve for Spurs in the replay, though, beaten 1-0 at Carrow Road.

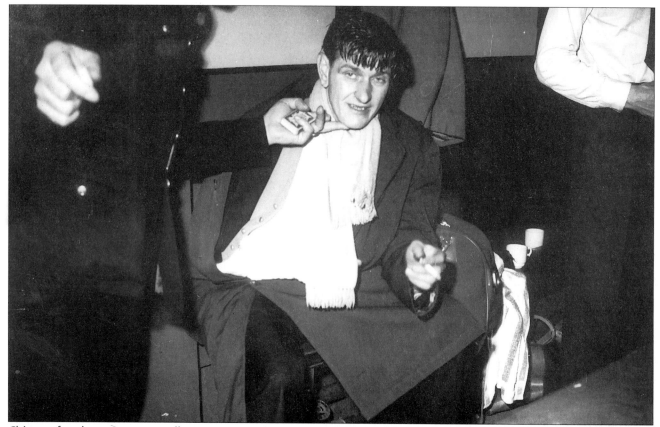

Chin up for the camera – goalkeeper Ken Nethercott, his right arm in a sling, waits to make the homeward trip to Norwich after his bravery helped earn the Canaries a quarter-final replay against Sheffield United. Dislocating his shoulder after diving at the feet of United's Hamilton, Nethercott played on for the last half-hour rather than leave City a man short, during which time Errol Crossan scored the equaliser which secured a replay.

Crowds for City's 11 FA Cup matches in 1958-59 totalled more than 430,000, and 57,000 of them were at Bramall Lane for the quarter-final against Sheffield United. With City attacking here, United goalkeeper Alan Hodgkinson punches clear under pressure from Terry Allcock (8).

Sandy Kennon was thrust unexpectedly into the spotlight when Ken Nethercott dislocated his shoulder in City's FA Cup quarter-final tie against Sheffield United at Bramall Lane. On trial at Carrow Road after being given a free transfer by Huddersfield, Kennon was pitched straight into the replay four days later. But he came through the unnerving experience, performed heroically in the two semi-final matches against Luton, and went on to make 255 first-team appearances up to 1964.

City fans donned all sorts of extraordinary attire to add a dash of colour to the great FA Cup campaign, with mascots, placards, cut-out cups and, in this instance, even a caged bird on display. 'You Blades are not sharp enough to cut our Canary', reads the placard on the left, before the quarter-final replay against Sheffield United at Carrow Road. How true, for City won 3-2 to reach the semi-finals.

Each of City's FA Cup home matches of 1959, from the third round onwards, was watched by capacity 38,000 crowds. And one look at the sea of heads here shows how they packed on to the popular terrace along the side of the ground which became covered in the early 1960s as the South Stand. The action comes from the first half of the quarter-final

replay against Sheffield United, with City attacking the River End goal. Terry Allcock (left) and Terry Bly are the Norwich players, with Alan Hodgkinson in goal for the Blades. Remarkably, Hodgkinson was still playing for United against the Canaries in the early 1970s.

Something rather stronger than the traditional dressing-room cuppa was on offer after City booked their place in the FA Cup semi-finals for the first time. Errol Crossan (left) and Terry Bly have good reason to celebrate after the 3-2 quarter-final replay victory over Sheffield United, in which Bly scored twice.

A collectors' item – the programme for City's FA Cup semi-final against Luton at White Hart Lane in 1959. The aerial view of the ground was a popular cover design, and one which the Canaries used themselves.

TOTTENHAM HOTSPUR FOOTBALL AND ATHLETIC COMPANY LIMITED

AERIAL VIEW OF THE SPURS GROUND

FOOTBALL ASSOCIATION CHALLENGE CUP

SEMI-FINAL TIE

SATURDAY, MARCH 14th, 1959

LUTON TOWN
v.
NORWICH CITY

Kick-off 3.30 p.m.

THE OFFICIAL **6**D. PROGRAMME

First-half action from the Canaries' semi-final meeting with Luton at White Hart Lane as goalkeeper Sandy Kennon gathers the ball under pressure from Luton inside-right Alan Brown, with City centre-half Barry Butler (right) in close attendance. Brown scored the Hatters' goal in a 1-1 draw.

The one that got away – Luton go 1-0 up in the semi-final at White Hart Lane as Alan Brown, out of picture, converts a centre from Billy Bingham. The Canary quartet looking anxiously on are (left to right) Matt Crowe, Barry Butler, Bryan Thurlow and goalkeeper Sandy Kennon.

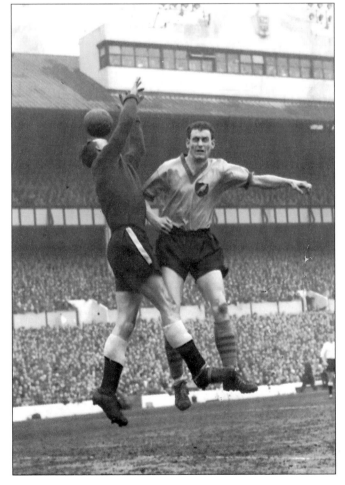

Semi-final action from White Hart Lane as Terry Allcock challenges Luton goalkeeper Ron Baynham for a high ball during a second half attack by the Canaries. A goal from Bobby Brennan earned City a replay at St Andrew's, Birmingham, four days later.

Lucky escape for Luton as City's Errol Crossan heads the ball home for what, for a brief moment, looked like the equaliser at White Hart Lane. The 'goal' was disallowed, much to the relief of the Hatters, whose goalkeeper Ron Baynham is stranded beyond the far post while skipper Sid Owen (third from left) looks on. The Canaries later levelled through birthday boy Bobby Brennan.

Luton goalkeeper Ron Baynham has plenty of cover here during a City attack in the FA Cup semi-final at White Hart Lane. Jimmy Hill is the Norwich forward on the six-yard line, waiting to cash in on any mistake. Note the battery of Press photographers on the far side of Baynham's goal, anxious not to miss any of the Canaries' remarkable exploits against First Division opponents.

There was no shortage of good luck greetings for the heroic City side on their way to the FA Cup semi-finals in 1959 – and never more appropriately than on 14 March when they faced Luton. It was left winger Bobby Brennan's 35th birthday and he celebrated by scoring the goal which gave City a replay. In this picture he is seen reading birthday telegrams in the dressing-room after the match.

The old master and the new recruit discuss the finer points of goalkeeping in the dressing-room at White Hart Lane after City's FA Cup semi-final against Luton. Sandy Kennon (left) was applauded for his acrobatic performance against the Hatters. Kennon had replaced Ken Nethercott (right) in the previous round. Nethercott, one of City's all-time greats, played for the last half an hour in the quarter-final at Sheffield United with a dislocated shoulder. Sadly, it proved to be his final first-team match for the club.

Goalkeeper Kennon safely clutches the ball after cutting out a centre during the semi-final replay against Luton at St Andrew's. Skipper Ron Ashman (3) guards the post.

The end of City's FA Cup dream came 56 minutes into their semi-final replay against Luton at St Andrew's. Kennon makes a desperate leap but is unable to stop Billy Bingham's shot from flashing into the net for the winning goal. Norwich defenders Roy McCrohan (left) and Bryan Thurlow look on helplessly. For them, it is the end of the road to Wembley.

Seldom can a losing side have been welcomed back with such fervour as the Canaries after their semi-final defeat by Luton. Crowds at Thorpe Station gathered to cheer their heroes home, as they had done throughout their extraordinary bid to reach Wembley. Skipper Ron Ashman (back to camera) conducts his team in a chorus or two, as supporters jostle for a view of their idols.

Spirit in the City camp clearly didn't suffer lasting damage despite the heartbreaking nature of their semi-final exit. The musical trio just in front of the W.H.Smith bookstall are (left to right): Roy McCrohan, Terry Allcock and Sandy Kennon, with Matt Crowe tucked in behind them. Despite a backlog of matches which forced them to play 16 times in less than six weeks before the end of the season, they were beaten only twice and finished fourth in Division Three.

The Swinging Sixties

IT MAY have been the decade of social revolution and great cultural change, but for Norwich City the 1960s was mostly a time of frustration and, after initial joy at reaching Division Two, stagnation.

The Canaries followed up their FA Cup exploits under Archie Macaulay with long-awaited promotion in 1960 as runners-up to Southampton in Division Three.

And so naturally did they take to life in a higher division that they were knocking on the door to Division One for much of the 1960-61 season, eventually finishing fourth.

Even after the untimely departure of manager Macaulay to West Bromwich Albion in October 1961, City managed to land some silverware under new boss Willie Reid, becoming the second winners of the Football League Cup in May 1962 with a 4-0 aggregate success over Rochdale.

However, Reid and his successor, George Swindin, stayed only briefly in the Carrow Road hot seat and the managerial post passed to City's veteran skipper, Ron Ashman, for three and a half seasons.

City's best performance under Ashman came in 1964-65, when they were placed sixth in Division Two, but a year later he was dismissed and the rest of the decade was one of mixed fortunes as Lol Morgan attempted to mould the Canaries into a force capable of challenging for promotion. In spite of considerable investment, it was an elusive dream.

At least City maintained their reputation as Cup fighters throughout the 1960s. They fairly stormed into the FA Cup quarter-finals in a flurry of matches in 1963, when a severe winter was followed by an equally severe backlog of games. But Leicester City ended thoughts of Wembley as their quarter-final at Carrow Road brought a new crowd record.

In 1967 came arguably the Canaries' most remarkable FA Cup win of all, a 2-1 triumph against Manchester United at Old Trafford. The following season, they accounted for Sunderland before losing at Chelsea.

The 1960s also brought some great individual players and characters to Norwich as fans marvelled at the finishing of Ron Davies and Hugh Curran, the artistry of Tommy Bryceland and the acrobatics of goalkeeper Kevin Keelan.

City made no great improvement in status as they hovered either side of mid-table, but they had their moments, and the man to break them out of this run of disappointments was waiting in the wings.

The winning momentum which took City to the brink of a Wembley Final in 1959 was carried into the following Division Three campaign and in April 1960 they clinched promotion, finishing second behind Southampton. A goalless draw at Queen's Park Rangers on 23 April all but guaranteed the Canaries promotion, but they made sure with a 4-3 home win in the next match against Southend. The players pictured in the dressing-room after the Rangers match are (standing, left to right): Bunny Larkin, Bobby Brennan, Matt Crowe, Roy McCrohan, Jimmy Hill, Bryan Thurlow, Sandy Kennon (partly hidden), and (foreground) Barry Butler (partly hidden), Terry Allcock.

Willie Reid took over as City manager in December 1961, but his stay was a short one. He had been connected with St Mirren for 17 years as player, trainer and manager and was one of nine men interviewed for the Carrow Road job. He stayed only five months, but in that time, the Canaries knocked Ipswich Town – on their way to the League title – out of the FA Cup and won the Football League Cup with a 4-0 aggregate success over Rochdale. Their final position of 17th in Division Two was less impressive and Reid returned to Scotland at the end of the season.

If Ipswich Town have had the upper hand over the Canaries in League meetings over the years, City have certainly had the better of local derbies in Cup competitions. And one of their finest successes of all came in the FA Cup fourth round in 1962, when City won 2-1 in a replay at Portman Road after a 1-1 draw at Carrow Road in front of a 39,890 crowd. Terry Allcock scored all three goals for Norwich, and a measure of their achievement was the fact that Town went on to win the League championship. In this picture, from the Carrow Road tie, goalkeeper Sandy Kennon is challenged by Ray Crawford. City players looking on are (left to right) Ron Ashman, Barry Butler, Allcock and Joe Mullett.

Stanley Matthews had just celebrated his 47th birthday when he played for Stoke City against the Canaries at Carrow Road on 10 February 1962. His presence, coupled with the clamour for FA Cup tickets for City's fifth-round tie at Sheffield United the following week, swelled the gate to 31,304. But the Matthews magic didn't work wonders for Stoke. A second-half goal from Terry Allcock gave Norwich both points.

The days of five forwards began to disappear in the 1960s, but this picture from February 1962 was obviously intended to capture the City forward line of the day in 7 to 11 order. They are (left to right): Gerry Mannion, the England Under-23 winger signed from Wolves; Terry Allcock, who was one of City's key players throughout the decade; Jim Conway, the crew-cut Scot signed from Celtic; Jimmy Hill, Northern Ireland international and another of the stars of 1959; and Derrick Lythgoe, who scored twice in the first leg of City's League Cup Final victory over Rochdale in 1962, and whose son Phil played for the Canaries in the late 1970s.

This was the age of the train – at least it was for Norwich City players travelling to a big match. Ron Ashman (left) and Barry Butler take their seats for the trip to Sheffield in February 1962, where the Canaries faced United in an FA Cup fifth-round tie at Bramall Lane. They are pictured reading special souvenir editions of the soccer paper, the *Pink 'Un*, which forecast a repeat of the thrilling 1959 win over the Blades. This time, however, City were beaten 3-1.

Gordon Banks made many a more famous save than this, but his greatest years were still to come when he appeared for Leicester City in front of Carrow Road's all-time record crowd of 43,984 on 30 March 1963. The occasion was an FA Cup quarter-final, but despite a mood of optimism among the capacity crowd, Leicester won 2-0 with goals from Mike Stringfellow and Dave Gibson and went on to reach Wembley, where they were beaten 3-1 by Manchester United. Banks is seen here leaping high in the Barclay End goalmouth, with Terry Allcock closing in. Note the way the fans are crammed into the South Stand, some standing in front of the perimeter fence.

It's three against two as City pair Terry Allcock and Jimmy Hill find themselves outnumbered by Leicester defenders, including a youthful Frank McLintock (second from left) during the FA Cup quarter-final at Carrow Road in 1963. Like the rest of the ground, the open River End terrace was jam-packed as City's record crowd paid more than £8,000 to see the match.

City had beaten Blackpool, Newcastle and Manchester City in some style to reach the last eight of the FA Cup in 1963, but that was the end of the glory trail. Goalkeeper Sandy Kennon is up against goalscorer Dave Gibson here in this shot from the 2-0 quarter-final defeat at the hands of Leicester at Carrow Road. It was to be another 20 years before the Canaries reached the quarter-finals of the competition, when they lost 1-0 at Brighton.

This marvellous City team shot, taken during the 1963-64 season, includes faces which span six decades in the club's history. Billy Furness (standing, extreme left) signed as a player in 1937 and was still serving the club in an off-field capacity when this picture was taken. Manager Ron Ashman (seated, centre) made his City debut in 1947 and had only just hung up his boots to concentrate on management after a year as acting manager. Goalkeeper Kevin Keelan was in his first season here, but did not play his last senior match for City until 9 February 1980. Back row (left to right): Terry Allcock, Gerry Mannion, Ken Hill, Sandy Kennon, Barry Butler, Kevin Keelan, Fred Sharpe, Joe Mullett, Bill Punton. Front row: Billy Furness, Phil Kelly, Tommy Bryceland, Mike Sutton, Ron Ashman (manager), Jim Oliver, Ron Barnes, Ron Davies, George Lee (trainer). Seated on ground: Colin Worrell and Jackie Bell.

The first of many Welsh international caps for centre-forward Ron Davies after his debut for his country against the Irish in 1964. "I hope you will win many more of these," City chairman Geoffrey Watling told Davies as he presented him with his cap in the boardroom. Indeed he did – 29 in all.

Most City fans lucky enough to have seen Ron Davies in Canary colours regard him as the finest centre-forward ever to play for the club. With the help of a £20,000 donation from the Supporters' Club – tireless contributors to the club coffers in that period – City splashed out a record £35,000 to bring him to Carrow Road from Luton in September 1963. And they were handsomely repaid as the Welshman rattled in 66 goals for the Canaries in only 126 senior games. There was an outcry when he was sold to Southampton in 1966 for £60,000. Davies won a total of 29 full Welsh caps and was once dubbed the finest centre-forward in Europe by Sir Matt Busby. Davies is pictured (right) in aerial combat with Blackburn centre-half Mike England in an FA Cup-tie at Carrow Road in 1966. Davies and England were at school together and went on to play for Wales together. Dave Stringer (2) is in close attendance.

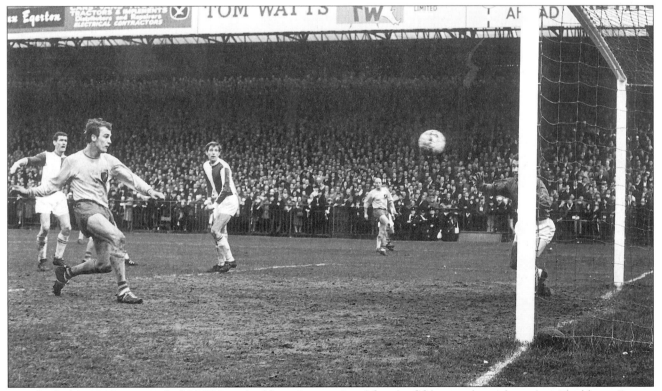

A typically big FA Cup crowd of 30,751 packed into Carrow Road for the fifth-round match against Blackburn Rovers on 5 March 1966. Ron Davies scored both goals in a 2-2 draw, but City lost the replay 3-2 at Ewood Park. Rovers goalkeeper Fred Else is powerless to stop Davies, while teammates Ronnie Clayton (left) and Keith Newton look on. In the background is City winger Bill Punton.

Above: Under suitably sombre skies, Carrow Road paid tribute to one of its all-time greats when a minute's silence was held before the home game against Rotherham United on Monday, 11 April 1966. Two days earlier, club captain Barry Butler had been killed in a car crash – a shattering blow for all connected with the club. Butler played 349 times for City between 1957 and 1965. Both teams wore black armbands for the Second Division match. The City team (right to left) was Hugh Curran (substitute), Fred Sharpe, Gordon Bolland, Ron Davies, Mal Lucas, Tommy Bryceland, Don Heath, Bill Punton, Dave Stringer, Joe Mullett, goalkeeper Kevin Keelan and team captain Terry Allcock.

Below: Even the brilliance of George Best could not prevent another of City's glorious FA Cup triumphs in 1967. Fourth-round day, Saturday, 18 February, took the Canaries to Old Trafford to meet mighty Manchester United, who included Best, Denis Law and England World Cup winners Bobby Charlton and Nobby Stiles in their line-up. Against all the odds, Second Division strugglers City beat United 2-1 with goals from Don Heath and Gordon Bolland.

Best gets in a cross here, watched by City's Terry Allcock (left) and Joe Mullett.

Lol Morgan, a former full-back with Huddersfield, Rotherham and Darlington, succeeded Ron Ashman as City manager in June 1966 at the age of 35. He had managed Darlington to promotion and it was hoped he could do the same for Norwich. But the Canaries could do no better than 11th, ninth and 13th in Division Two in his three seasons in charge, despite considerable outlay in the transfer market. Some of his signings proved excellent servants for City – men such as Duncan Forbes, Ken Foggo and Alan Black. Other investments, such as a club record £40,000 for his cousin Ken Mallender from Sheffield United, and £25,000 for wing-half Gerry Howshall from West Bromwich Albion, were less successful. Highlights of Morgan's managerial reign came in Cup competitions, with FA Cup victories over First Division sides Manchester United and Sunderland and a stunning League Cup win over Ipswich at Portman Road.

Laurie Brown heads clear under challenge from Denis Law during City's 2-1 FA Cup triumph at Old Trafford. Teammates (left to right) Mal Lucas, Terry Allcock and Mike Kenning provide support in numbers. Brown, an England amateur international, represented Great Britain at the 1960 Olympic Games in Rome. He also had spells with both North London giants, Arsenal and Tottenham.

They shall not pass... Laurie Brown hammers the ball clear during another United attack, with Kevin Keelan guarding his post and Joe Mullett looking on. The United players are Denis Law (left) and Jim Ryan.

The look of concern on the face of Nobby Stiles (far right) is more than justified – for City are about to take a decisive 2-1 lead at Old Trafford in the FA Cup fourth-round tie. An attempted back-pass from United full-back Tony Dunne eludes goalkeeper Alex Stepney, and City's Gordon Bolland is ready to pounce and knock in the winning goal.

It must have been one of the easiest goals Gordon Bolland ever scored, but for City fans, it was the goal of the decade! Bolland knocks in the winner against Manchester United to complete a shock win – and 63,405 were there to see it.

Local derbies against Ipswich Town have provided their share of nail-biting action over the years, and one of the classics was staged at Carrow Road on 3 February 1968. Town won 4-3 and went on to clinch the Second Division championship at the end of the season. But City, who had drawn 0-0 at Portman Road early in the season, gave them an almighty scare in the return meeting, going 2-0 up through Hugh Curran and Charlie Crickmore. Curran is pictured racing away after opening the scoring.

The Barry Butler Memorial Trophy was introduced in 1967 by club chairman Geoffrey Watling for City's Player of the Year. First winner in the supporters' poll was Terry Allcock, pictured here receiving his award from Mr Watling after the final home match of 1966-67, against Northampton.

A packed South Stand – part of a crowd of 30,184 – provides the backdrop as Charlie Crickmore fires the Canaries into a 2-0 lead over Ipswich in the local derby of 1968 at Carrow Road. Town hit back to win 4-3. It was Crickmore's home debut for City after a £15,000 move from Rotherham and he went on to score ten goals in 64 senior games for City on the left wing.

Celebrations all round as Charlie Crickmore (11) is congratulated by John Manning, with Hugh Curran (10) waiting to salute the goalscorer. Skipper Laurie Brown (second from right, in distance) indulges in more extravagant celebrations of his own as City – note the clock on the South Stand – take a 2-0 lead inside 25 minutes against Ipswich.

Hugh Curran heads City's third goal against Ipswich on 3 February 1968, but they were already 4-2 down thanks mainly to a hat-trick by Town's Colin Viljoen. Curran finished the season with 18 goals and was voted Player of the Year. He added a further 22 goals in 31 games the following season, including a League Cup hat-trick in a 4-2 win at Ipswich, before he was sold to Wolves for £60,000.

The FA Cup trail took the Canaries to Chelsea on fourth-round day on 17 February 1968, a year after their famous triumph in the same round at Old Trafford. But this time, the First Division club squeezed home 1-0, thanks to a first-half goal by Charlie Cooke at Stamford Bridge. Cooke is hidden by happy teammates (left to right) Bobby Tambling, Ron Harris, Peter Osgood and John Hollins after scoring. The dejected Canaries (left to right) are John Manning, Mal Lucas and, retrieving the ball from the back of the net, goalkeeper Kevin Keelan.

The architecture of Stamford Bridge has changed a good deal since the late 1960s. Here it provides the backdrop for FA Cup action as Chelsea players (left to right) Bobby Tambling, Charlie Cooke, Tommy Baldwin and Peter Osgood celebrate Cooke's fourth-round winner over City on 17 February 1968. Disappointment shows among City trio (left to right) Laurie Brown, Mal Lucas and Fred Sharpe.

City defend in depth against Chelsea in the FA Cup at Stamford Bridge. Goalkeeper Kevin Keelan comes out to thwart Tommy Baldwin (8) and the other Canaries are (left to right) Dave Stringer, Alan Black, Fred Sharpe, Laurie Brown, Charlie Crickmore and Ken Foggo.

Alan Black heads clear during a Chelsea attack, watched anxiously by teammates Fred Sharpe (left) and Dave Stringer, with Chelsea's Bobby Tambling (left) and Peter Osgood looking on. Black and Stringer had happier times to come at Stamford Bridge. Four years later, they were in the City team who won a League Cup semi-final first leg match on the same ground on the way to Wembley.

The signing of Duncan Forbes on 12 September 1968, represented arguably the best £10,000 Norwich City ever spent. Forbes, an indestructible Scot, joined the Canaries from Colchester and went on to make a total of 357 senior appearances for the club over the next 12 years, making his farewell appearance at the age of 39. An iron man at centre-half, Forbes led City to promotion twice and to two Wembley Finals, and suffered a string of injuries which might have broken lesser men, including a punctured lung in a League Cup quarter-final triumph at Arsenal in 1972. Player of the Year in 1970, Forbes clocked up 25 years at Carrow Road in 1993, working for the promotions department then as chief scout after hanging up his boots.

Lol Morgan's reign as manager was nearing its end when this City team picture was taken in December 1968, but some of the players he left behind were to play a key role in the successes of the early 1970s under Ron Saunders. Morgan was asked to resign the following April following a 4-1 home defeat by Brian Clough's Derby County. Back row (left to right): Ken Foggo, Trevor Howard, Gerry Howshall, Dave Stringer, Kevin Keelan, Terry Anderson, Geoff Butler. Front row: Neil O'Donnell, John Manning, Ken Mallender, Hugh Curran, Duncan Forbes.

Into the Big Time

LITTLE in City's performances during Ron Saunders' first two seasons in charge at Carrow Road suggested that they were about to take Division Two by the scruff of the neck in 1971-72.

They had acquired a certain solidity in defence and showed commendable industry in midfield, but the style of football favoured by Saunders met with a lukewarm reception from supporters who viewed it as too negative to bring City any tangible reward. How wrong can you get?

By the summer of 1972, Saunders and his side were local heroes as they booked City a place in Division One for the first time in club history, winning a tense battle for the Second Division championship by a single point from Birmingham City.

They had also brought the fans flooding back to Carrow Road, eager to be part of the great promotion party after years of false hope.

So it was that the Canaries, their challenge fronted by club stalwarts such as Kevin Keelan, Dave Stringer and Duncan Forbes and given new invention by shrewd acquisitions like Graham Paddon, David Cross and Jim Bone, strode boldly on to the First Division stage in August 1972.

Swept on by the momentum of their championship campaign, they toppled some of the big names in Derby, Arsenal and Tottenham in the early weeks of the season, and set off on a remarkable League Cup campaign that was to take them to Wembley after much drama taking the scalps of Arsenal and Chelsea.

Even if Wembley brought defeat by Spurs, and the League campaign became a grim struggle for survival – ultimately successful only with an injury-time winner in the final home game against Crystal Palace – there was hope that Saunders would be able to establish City on a firmer top-flight footing in 1973-74.

What followed was a major disappointment as City struggled almost from the word go, and a frustrated Saunders, at loggerheads with the chairman, resigned in November 1973, by which time his team were facing more than an uphill battle to survive.

So ended the Saunders revolution at Norwich. But an even more radical overhaul was in the offing.

Ron Saunders, indisputably one of the best managers in Norwich City history, was appointed on 10 July 1969. Within three years, he had achieved his aim of getting the club into Division One, a year sooner than he had expected. And in 1973, he took them to Wembley for the first time in the League Cup Final. Saunders was 36 when he became City boss. Although his Football League playing career took him to Everton, Gillingham, Portsmouth, Watford and Charlton as a tough centre-forward, it was on the virtues of solid defence, super fitness and sheer hard work that he moulded his championship-winning City side. It was curious that the four men who followed him into the Carrow Road hot seat – Bond, Brown, Stringer and Walker – all fashioned more flamboyant, attacking sides, yet three were defenders and one a goalkeeper. Nevertheless, it was the Saunders reign which laid the foundations for City's rise in status in the 1970s through to the 1990s.

Arguably the most popular player with the Carrow Road crowd in the late 1960s and early 1970s, Ken Foggo was the first man to win two Player of the Year awards, topping the poll in both 1969 and 1971, and deservedly so. A goalscoring winger, Foggo was top scorer in City's Second Division championship team of 1971-72 with 13 goals in 38 League games. Signed from West Bromwich Albion for a bargain £15,000 in October 1967, the former Scottish schoolboy international chalked up a healthy total of 57 goals in 201 senior appearances for City. Sadly, for a player with such a key role in getting the Canaries into Division One, he was given only two brief outings as a substitute in the top flight before being sold to Portsmouth in January 1973 for £25,000.

Ron Saunders placed tremendous emphasis on the fitness of his players and it proved a key element in the Canaries' success. Here skipper Duncan Forbes goes through the traditional rigours of a run over Mousehold Heath – far too preoccupied to appreciate a panoramic view of Norwich. Saunders even introduced a 'sweat box' in his later days at Carrow Road, a move which brought criticism from those who felt the more subtle side of the game was being neglected.

Carrow Road staged a classic promotion battle on 12 February 1972, when City took on Millwall in front of more than 34,000 fans. The Canaries were top of Division Two with the Lions in second place, and a tense encounter ended 2-2. While City went on to championship glory, Millwall were pipped for the second promotion spot by Birmingham City. Pictured are two of the key players in the engine room of Ron Saunders' championship side, Doug Livermore (left) and Graham Paddon. Injury curtailed Livermore's top-class career but he went on to play for Cardiff and Chester before taking coaching posts at Cardiff, Norwich, Swansea, Tottenham and Liverpool, where he began his career. Paddon moved to West Ham in 1973, securing an FA Cup winners' medal in 1975 and returning to Norwich in 1976 for a further five years, making a total of 340 senior appearances for the club.

The signing of Jim Bone from Partick Thistle gave fresh impetus to City's promotion challenge. The £30,000 striker is pictured in action on his home debut for the Canaries against Sunderland on 11 March 1972. Bone scored City's equaliser in a 1-1 draw and went on to score three more times before the end of a triumphant season. He then had the honour of netting Norwich's first-ever goal in Division One, in a 1-1 draw against Everton at Carrow Road on the opening day of the 1972-73 campaign. In all, Bone scored 15 times in 51 appearances for City, but was transferred to Sheffield United in the part exchange deal which brought Trevor Hockey to Carrow Road. The move was something of a shock to City fans coming only ten days before their League Cup Final meeting with Tottenham.

The Canaries saved their most emphatic display of the 1971-72 championship campaign for the visit of Blackpool on Saturday, 25 March. City triumphed 5-1 – indeed, they were 4-1 ahead at half-time – and it was a result which lifted Ron Saunders' team out of an indifferent spell and put them in fine fettle for the final run-in to promotion. Skipper Duncan Forbes is pictured heading clear in a rare Blackpool attack, while full-back Clive Payne provides extra cover.

There was rarely a more popular winner of the Barry Butler Memorial Trophy, City's Player of the Year award, than Dave Stringer in 1972. Born at Southtown, Great Yarmouth, he made his debut in 1965 for the Canaries and spent the early years of his career at right-back. But it was his central defensive partnership with Duncan Forbes during the Saunders and Bond managerial years which proved the cornerstone of so many successes for City. Stringer captained City for long spells during Forbes' absence with injury in both 1971-72 and 1972-73 seasons and made a total of 499 appearances, scoring 22 goals, before moving to Cambridge United in 1976. Stringer returned to Carrow Road as youth-team boss, leading the side to the South East Counties League and FA Youth Cup double in 1983, and of course, had four and a half years as first-team manager.

The Canaries clinched promotion to Division One for the first time with a 2-1 win at Orient on Monday, 24 April 1972. It was Ken Foggo's goal which broke the ice and here Foggo's shot is on its way past Orient goalkeeper Ray Goddard to put City 1-0 up. A crowd of 15,530 packed into Brisbane Road, most of them having made the trip from Norfolk, and there were some great celebrations on the way home.

David Cross, arms aloft, is jubilant as the ball nestles in the net. Ken Foggo has just put City ahead against Orient at Brisbane Road and the expressions of the two Orient men say it all. City's 2-1 win left them needing only a point from their final match at Watford to secure the championship.

Dressing-room celebrations were soon in full swing after City's win at Orient clinched promotion to Division One. Trainer George Lee is ready to give Graham Paddon a champagne shampoo, with fellow goalscorer Ken Foggo (right) about to get the same treatment.

£

RECEIVED

TELEGRAM

Prefix. Time handed in.   Office of Origin and Service Instructions.   Words.

At_____ m

G6   N236   19.30   BUCKINGHAM PALACE   51 By

LORD MAYOR OF NORWICH CITY HALL NORWICH

= I AM DELIGHTED THAT NORWICH HAVE TODAY BECOME CHAMPIONS OF THE SECOND DIVISION . PLEASE CONVEY MY WARMEST CONGRATULATIONS TO THEIR MANAGER AND TO ALL MEMBERS OF THE TEAM AND MY BEST WISHES FOR NEXT SEASON IN THE FIRST DIVISION = ELIZABETH R QUEEN MOTHER

For free repetition of doubtful ...   ...GRAMS ENQUIRY" or call, with this form
                                                                               B or C

City's success in winning the Second Division championship earned Royal approval, as this telegram from the Queen Mother proves. It was sent immediately after the Canaries' 1-1 draw at Watford, which clinched the title, and is further evidence of the Royal Family's special link with Norfolk through Sandringham. Some 34 years earlier, her husband, King George VI, had visited Carrow Road as the first reigning monarch to attend a Second Division match.

Who better than Dave Stringer (extreme left) to score the goal which clinched the Second Division championship at Watford? A crowd of 22,421 packed into Vicarage Road and despite dismal weather, there was a carnival atmosphere among the City followers as their heroes – wearing a change strip of all-red – earned a 1-1 draw against a Watford side whose battling display belied the fact that they were already relegated. Here Stringer heads City's goal past goalkeeper Andy Rankin, then celebrates with Max Briggs (left) and Jim Bone.

City's Second Division champions enjoy their moment of glory at Vicarage Road. The five faces visible at the front are (left to right) Max Briggs, Doug Livermore, Kevin Keelan (partly hidden), Terry Anderson and Dave Stringer, with Duncan Forbes, turning away, on the extreme right.

Celebration time for the Canaries and their thousands of followers as Duncan Forbes holds the Second Division championship trophy aloft on the balcony of City Hall after the team's triumphant parade through Norwich at the end of the 1971-72 season.

Travelling in style into Division One – the squad which won the Second Division championship in 1972. Seated in the front of the car (left to right) are manager Ron Saunders, captain Duncan Forbes and vice-captain Dave Stringer. In the back (left to right) are Jim Bone, Kevin Keelan and Terry Anderson. Standing (left to right) are Clive Payne, Geoff Butler, Trevor Howard, Doug Livermore, Ken Foggo, Alan Black, Graham Paddon, Phil Hubbard, Steve Govier, Peter Silvester, David Cross, Mervyn Cawston and Max Briggs.

Arguably the most unusual team picture in City's history was taken at the Norwood Rooms in May 1972 as the Second Division championship-winning squad recorded their own disc. *The Canaries* was described on the sleeve as 'one of the best football songs to be heard to date'. Loyalty forbids a more discerning appraisal, but fans queued at shops across the county for signed copies. The *Norwich City Calypso* formed the 'B' side of the record. Both songs were written by Don Shepherd and Johnny Cleveland, keen City fans and members of the Chic Applin Band. Alas, it failed to dislodge T.Rex from the top of the charts.

An historic moment at Carrow Road as Duncan Forbes leads out the Canaries for their first-ever game in Division One against Everton on Saturday, 12 August 1972. City were puzzled by the attendance of only 26,028, more than 10,000 below capacity for such a notable occasion. But crowds soon picked up as Saunders' men began the campaign brightly.

First blood to Norwich as Jim Bone scores the Canaries' first-ever Division One goal against Everton. It gave them a 1-0 interval lead but a late equaliser by Joe Royle took the edge off the celebrations. Bone's teammates pictured are David Cross (left) and Max Briggs, while the Everton quartet are John McLaughlan, goalkeeper David Lawson, Mike Lyons and Howard Kendall.

Delight on the Barclay terrace and for Jim Bone after his goal against Everton. Bone is about to be congratulated by Doug Livermore (7) with David Cross (left) and Clive Payne (right) completing the picture. Note the absence of the canary badge from City's shirts. It was in the process of being redesigned and reappeared later in the season in a design which survives today.

City's first season in Division One fired the imagination of the fans and the average home attendance reached a new record 28,652. The visit of Liverpool for example, in October 1972 attracted an attendance of 36,590 as Norwich supporters jumped at the chance to see the big names of British football on a regular basis. This picture shows the packed South Stand and River End corner as City's Jim Bone finds himself well policed by Liverpool's Larry Lloyd (right) and Alec Lindsay.

City's League Cup semi-final against Chelsea in 1972-73 delivered the most extraordinary drama, but little did anyone envisage such a nerve-jangling time when the Canaries cruised to a 2-0 win in the first leg at Stamford Bridge. David Cross, who scored City's first goal, is pictured just missing out on a high ball into the Chelsea area.

Getting to know you… the Canaries became very closely acquainted with Chelsea in the winter of 1972-73, meeting them four times in the space of 25 days in December and January. In the first meeting, on 9 December, City lost 3-1 at Stamford Bridge in a Division One encounter. David Cross is outnumbered here by Chelsea trio (left to right) David Webb, Bill Garner and Micky Droy. Four days later, City went back to Stamford Bridge and won 2-0 in the first leg of their League Cup semi-final.

The Canaries were well on their way to Wembley by the time Jim Bone tucked away the second goal in their League Cup semi-final first leg at Chelsea. Two goals up with the home leg to come... what could possibly stop them?

The second leg of City's semi-final against Chelsea provided a night of drama the 32,000 crowd will never forget. The Canaries moved into a 3-2 lead in a see-saw game, 5-2 ahead on aggregate, when thick fog enveloped the ground, forcing the game to be abandoned with less than six minutes remaining. Terry Anderson (11) is pictured scoring Norwich's first goal, with the ground already shrouded in fog.

David Cross (9) is congratulated by Paul Cheesley after scoring City's second goal in the fogged-off match against Chelsea. Cheesley, just 19, scored the third goal in the Canaries' 3-2 win, but the whole match was rendered null and void.

Referee Gordon Hill (second from left) had to take the unenviable decision to abandon City's semi-final, second leg with only six minutes left. Despite one brief attempt to restart the match, it was impossible to carry on. City manager Ron Saunders (left) looks suitably grim-faced, but for Chelsea boss Dave Sexton (right), there was an unexpected second chance to make up the two-goal deficit.

It all came right for City when the second leg against Chelsea was replayed on Wednesday, 3 January 1973, and a 1-0 win took them to Wembley by a 3-0 aggregate. This was the goal which settled the second leg as centre-half Steve Govier (right of the jumping pair, the other is Dave Stringer) heads home, to the delight of a crowd of 34,265. Govier was deputising for injured skipper Duncan Forbes, but Forbes was back for the Final.

It's all over – and City match winner Steve Govier shakes hands with Chelsea's Chris Garland at the end of the League Cup semi-final marathon. Behind them, a handful of jubilant fans are already charging across the pitch.

Wembley was a piece of cake for the Canaries in 1973, despite their League Cup Final defeat by Tottenham. City chairman Geoffrey Watling had this Wembley cake baked specially for the after-match banquet, complete with Subbuteo-type figures representing opposing captains Duncan Forbes and Martin Peters. Mr Watling (right) proudly displays the cake, with club secretary Bert Westwood (left) and president James Hanly looking on.

City's first trip to Wembley ended in disappointment as they went down 1-0 to Tottenham in the 1973 League Cup Final. They had disposed of Arsenal and Chelsea in such heroic fashion in the quarter-final and semi-final that the Canary contingent travelled to the Final confident of another London scalp being added to the list. Alas, the Final came two months after the semi and Ron Saunders' side had gone off the boil and slipped into the relegation pack in Division One. Pictured here in a late, desperate attack, David Cross and Dave Stringer challenge Spurs goalkeeper Pat Jennings in the air, while Martin Peters (10) and Joe Kinnear (2) look on.

Beaten but not disgraced, City put on a brave face after their 1-0 defeat by Tottenham at Wembley, but the disappointment shows on the faces of manager Ron Saunders and skipper Duncan Forbes at the end of the match. When Forbes led the Canaries out at Wembley again two years later, Saunders was managing their opponents, Aston Villa.

Wembley must be the greatest place on earth for winners, and probably the worst place on earth for losers. This picture says it all as City, nearest the camera and clutching their losers' tankards, line up with Tottenham for the National Anthem after their 1-0 defeat in the League Cup Final of 1973. Skipper Duncan Forbes, in the foreground, stands proud and upright but the expressions of his colleagues convey their bitter disappointment. "I can always remember the band playing *Congratulations*," Dave Stringer once said. Alas, the message was for Spurs, in bright lights on the scoreboard.

Few players made so great an impact or achieved so much popularity in so short a space of time as did Trevor Hockey during his brief stay with the Canaries in 1973. He made only 13 first-team appearances for City after arriving at Carrow Road in a part-exchange deal which took striker Jim Bone to Sheffield United. But with a rugged approach in midfield which matched his appearance, the 5ft 6in powerhouse helped Ron Saunders' side stave off relegation from Division One. Hockey, born in Yorkshire, won nine caps for Wales and had spells coaching in America. City fans everywhere were saddened by his untimely death in 1987, at the age of 43, when he collapsed in his native Keighley following a five-a-side match.

Few goals at Carrow Road have sparked more emotional celebrations than these. Dave Stringer (second from left) has just headed an injury-time winner over Crystal Palace to save the Canaries from relegation to Division Two. A crowd of 36,922 – City's biggest of season 1972-73 – witnessed a gripping encounter, Stringer's goal sealing a 2-1 win which ultimately preserved Division One status for Norwich, if only for another year, and sent Palace down. Sharing the celebration (left to right) are skipper Duncan Forbes, Doug Livermore and Clive Payne.

Ron Saunders' fitness regime became even more exacting at the start of City's second season in Division One. He introduced the 'sweat box' at Trowse training ground, a 36-foot square wooden box, nine feet high with goal netting for a roof. The idea was for two players to kick a ball non-stop against the walls in a gruelling ten-minute session to sharpen up reflexes and maintain peak fitness. Doug Livermore (left) and Paul Cheesley are the unfortunate pair during this session, watched by trainer George Lee. When John Bond arrived midway through the season, he dispensed with the torture chamber and it was sold for timber the following summer.

The end of the road for Ron Saunders came on 17 November 1973, after City lost 3-1 at home to Everton in a bizarre match. Earlier kick-offs had been introduced because of a power crisis, and as if to underline the sense of unreality, all four goals were own goals, full-back Clive Payne was sent on as a substitute at centre-forward, and Saunders resigned after the game following a bitter boardroom row. In this picture, Paul Cheesley (9) challenges Everton goalkeeper David Lawson for a high ball as Dave Stringer (4) and Graham Paddon look on.

The Name's Bond

IF CITY had deliberately advertised for a manager completely the opposite of Ron Saunders in every sense, they could hardly have found a more suitable candidate than John Frederick Bond.

For nearly seven years under his guidance, the Canaries were committed to a brand of attacking football which made them one of the most attractive sides in the country.

At their best under Bond, City were breathtakingly brilliant. After winning promotion to Division One in 1975 with a team almost totally rebuilt by Bond in the space of 18 months, they became an established part of the First Division furniture, never in any real danger of going down but equally unlikely to win anything either, owing to the defensive frailty which went almost automatically with their adventurous style of play.

The Canaries flirted with European qualification during the Bond era, yet never finished higher than tenth, which in 1976 was no mean achievement in itself.

As manager, he brought top-class performers such as Martin Peters, Ted MacDougall and Kevin Reeves on to the Carrow Road stage and, more significantly, established a youth policy which was to produce future first-team regulars such as Peter Mendham, Mark Barham, Justin Fashanu and Paul Haylock.

City gained a much higher national profile during Bond's reign, not merely through their style of football, but also through his easy relationship with the media. There were few issues which did not get the Bond treatment and he was one of the more lively contributors to the BBC World Cup panel in the summer of 1978.

There were, equally, times when his outspokenness incurred the wrath of others in the game and may, inadvertently, have put pressure on his own team. Actions certainly spoke louder than words when Saunders' Aston Villa beat Bond's Canaries at Wembley in the 1975 League Cup Final.

The signing of Peters, his former colleague at West Ham, was probably the best piece of business performed by Bond, though the capture of Reeves for £50,000 – sold three years later for £1 million – runs it close.

In the end, the seven-year itch took its toll on Bond and in October 1980, his enthusiasm for Norwich on the wane, he resigned to take over as manager of Manchester City.

Bond's public criticism of his successor, Ken Brown, following his departure, did not endear him to City followers and there were those who were pleased to see him go.

But he had done much to take City forward and, given some of the football his team produced, his years in office can largely be looked back on with a nostalgic glow.

John Bond breezed into Carrow Road in November 1973, bringing with him brash suits, big cigars, bright and breezy football and what seemed like most of the Bournemouth staff. It was all in marked contrast to the style of management favoured by his predecessor, Ron Saunders. Where Saunders was reticent with the Press, Bond rapidly acquired a reputation as 'Rentaquote'. While Saunders dressed soberly, Bond was a dedicated follower of fashion. If Saunders was careful how he spent City's hard-earned cash resources, Bond splashed out freely in his first year in charge. And while Saunders based his success on hard work, fitness and defensive solidity, Bond favoured a more attacking approach. But each contributed massively in his own way to establishing Norwich as a First Division club after the stagnation of the 1960s.

Mel Machin was one of the first arrivals of the John Bond era, and was to become a key figure in the Canaries' fortunes over the next 14 years. As a defender whose cultured style was not always appreciated at Carrow Road, he made 117 senior appearances for City before a knee injury forced him to retire. Three of his four goals for Norwich came in the second half of one match – a remarkable hat-trick at Nottingham Forest in October 1974. He went on to become reserve-team boss, then chief coach during the Ken Brown reign, when City were relegated twice, promoted twice and won the Milk Cup at Wembley. He resigned in 1987 and became team manager at Manchester City.

Striker Phil Boyer was one of John Bond's first acquisitions as City manager and a key ingredient in the more expansive style of football favoured by Bond when he replaced Ron Saunders as boss. Like so many of his era at Carrow Road, Boyer signed for City from Bournemouth and his renewed attacking partnership with Ted MacDougall gave the Canaries one of the most potent goalscoring combinations in the land. A study in perpetual motion, Boyer was less prolific a goalscorer than MacDougall but his tireless approach so often created the space in which his partner flourished. Boyer, a club record £145,000 signing in February 1974, scored 40 times in 140 senior outings for City before moving to Southampton in August 1977 – again teaming up with MacDougall. He won one international cap under Don Revie, becoming the first Norwich player to play for England while on the club's books.

Father and son teamed up at Carrow Road in the summer of 1974 when 17-year-old Kevin Bond joined the Canaries as an apprentice. Bond, tipped by his father as a future international – quite impartially, of course – went on to make his senior debut for City as a substitute at Leicester in April 1976, and became a first-team regular in the 1977-78 season. A full-back who switched to central defence, where he looked more at home, Bond junior was appointed captain in 1980 but moved to Seattle Sounders in February 1981, four months after his father quit Carrow Road for Manchester City. The two teamed up again at Maine Road in the summer of 1981. The young Bond made a total of 161 first-team appearances for City, scoring 14 goals, most of them from the penalty spot.

City produced some heroic performances on their way to the League Cup Final of 1975, none more so than in the semi-final, first leg against Manchester United at Old Trafford. A crowd of 58,010 watched a gripping 2-2 draw. Alex Stepney is pictured punching clear under pressure from Ted MacDougall, watched by City's Tony Powell (left), who scored the opening goal, and United full-back Alex Forsyth.

This was the moment which turned City's League Cup semi-final against Manchester United in their favour. With two minutes left in the first leg at Old Trafford and United leading 2-1, goalkeeper Alex Stepney and full-back Stewart Houston suffer an appalling mix-up, the ball sticks in the muddy goalmouth and Ted MacDougall is waiting to pounce to guide home the equaliser. MacDougall scored four times in four matches against his old club in the 1974-75 season.

Not the most spectacular goal ever scored at Carrow Road, but certainly one which sealed one of the great victories... Colin Suggett (centre) scores from close range to give the Canaries a 1-0 win over Manchester United at Carrow Road in the second leg of the 1975 League Cup semi-final. Phil Boyer (left) is on the floor and Dave Stringer is in close

attendance as Suggett's effort loops past grounded United goalkeeper Alex Stepney. City had drawn the first leg 2-2 at Old Trafford and so went through to Wembley 3-2 on aggregate. Both teams were promoted from Division Two the same season, United as champions and City in third place.

Three of Norwich City's greatest servants – who eventually chalked up more than 1,500 first-team appearances between them – got together for this picture in the build-up to the 1975 League Cup Final at Wembley. They were the only three survivors from the 1973 Wembley Final to play again two years later. Duncan Forbes (top), goalkeeper Kevin Keelan and Dave Stringer all performed with distinction as City lost 1-0 to Aston Villa. Few of their colleagues could say the same.

One look at the clothes tells a great deal about the two managers as flamboyant City boss John Bond leads his team out at Wembley against Aston Villa, managed by who else but Ron Saunders, looking distinctly more sober in attire. The 1975 League Cup competition brought Saunders his third successive appearance in the Final, each time managing a different club. After defeats with Norwich and Manchester City, it was third time lucky for Saunders as Villa won 1-0. The Canaries may have won the fashion competition but that was about all, Bond talking up a much better Final than his players produced.

The moment which decided the 1975 League Cup Final. City's Mel Machin dives to palm away a header from Villa's Chris Nicholl (second right) and concede a penalty. With only 12 minutes left, the Canaries are heading for another Wembley defeat. Both Machin and John Miller had been struggling with injuries before the match and the decision to play them hardly helped City's cause.

Heartbreak for City – and especially goalkeeper Kevin Keelan – as Ray Graydon hammers Villa's winning goal. Keelan dived to his right and managed to turn Graydon's spot-kick on to the post, but the rebound fell perfectly for the Villa man, who made no mistake second time. "It was just my misfortune that instead of bouncing off somewhere else, the ball went straight out to Graydon again and he had an easy task of knocking it in," said Keelan. "That was it. Another Wembley defeat."

Another loser's tankard for City goalkeeper Kevin Keelan as he walks off the Wembley turf after the 1975 League Cup Final, with manager John Bond close behind and John Miller (left) equally downcast. Keelan produced a magnificent display and deserved better reward. Miller, who had been struggling with a knee injury leading up to the Final, suffered a nightmare afternoon.

The Canaries made up for their poor Wembley showing by clinching promotion back to Division One at the first attempt, and they secured third spot behind Manchester United and Aston Villa with a 3-0 win at Portsmouth on Saturday, 26 April. The goals came from Mick McGuire, Martin Peters and Phil Boyer. Here, McGuire – kneeling – is congratulated by Ted MacDougall and Boyer, with Colin Suggett (left) and Peter Morris (extreme right) waiting to join the celebrations. Portsmouth finished sixth from bottom in Division Two.

The signing of Martin Peters for £40,000 from Tottenham in March 1975 was a master-stroke by John Bond. He played in the last ten matches of City's promotion campaign and his experience proved vital in those tense final weeks of the season. Peters scored the second goal in the 3-0 win at Portsmouth which sealed promotion and stayed a further five years with the club, scoring 50 times in all.

Pepsi all round for City after their victory at Portsmouth secured a quick return to top-flight football. Goalscorers (left to right) Martin Peters, Phil Boyer and Mick McGuire savour the moment in the dressing-room at Fratton Park. The Canaries' only rivals for third place, Sunderland, were beaten 2-0 at Aston Villa the same day – enough to settle the issue.

The champagne was flowing at Fratton Park after City's success, and director and former chairman Geoffrey Watling was among the dressing-room visitors. Skipper Duncan Forbes helps him to sample the taste of victory on another notable day in club history.

The Canaries prepared for the 1975-76 season with renewed optimism after winning promotion with no little style, and though they made no significant additions to their squad during the summer of 1975, their confidence was justified as they finished tenth in Division One the following April. Back row (left to right): John Bond (manager), Mel Machin, John Miller, Duncan Forbes, Roger Hansbury, Kevin Keelan, Martin Peters, Tony Powell, Dave Stringer, Doug Livermore, Ken Brown (assistant manager). Front row: Peter Morris, Colin Suggett, Billy Steele, Colin Sullivan, Steve Grapes, Mick McGuire, Phil Boyer. The only major addition to this line-up was defender David Jones, signed from Nottingham Forest in September 1975.

A classic picture from a classic match… Ted MacDougall celebrates the second of his three goals in City's 5-3 win over Aston Villa at Carrow Road on 23 August 1975. It was the Canaries' second home match of the season after returning to Division One under John Bond, and the scoreline helped soothe a lot of lingering pain from the previous season, when Villa beat City at Wembley in the League Cup Final and followed it up with a 4-1 win at Norwich in the final match of the season. MacDougall's deadly finishing brought him hat-tricks in successive home games against Villa and Everton, and he had 15 goals in all competitions before the end of September.

Possibly the most unexpected victory of the entire Bond era came at Anfield on 29 November 1975. City had lost much of their early-season sparkle and the previous week, had slipped to their third defeat in five home games when Newcastle won 2-1 at Carrow Road. However, Bond told *Match of the Day* viewers that they would go to Liverpool to attack, a policy which brought them a 3-1 win with goals from Colin Suggett, Martin Peters and Ted MacDougall. Goalscorer Suggett (hidden by No 8 MacDougall) is congratulated after opening the scoring. Liverpool's Ian Callaghan (left) and John Toshack trudge back for the kick-off.

A cheery – and snowy – welcome to Carrow Road for 19-year-old Kevin Reeves from City assistant manager Ken Brown. Reeves joined Norwich in January 1977 from Bournemouth, initially on loan, but a £50,000 fee made the move permanent the following month and he proved a bargain. Reeves scored 42 goals in 133 games for City and his cultured football earned him his first England cap against Bulgaria in 1979. In March 1980, he became City's first £1 million export, joining Manchester City. Manager John Bond followed seven months later and together they walked out of the Wembley tunnel for the FA Cup Final of 1981. Reeves scored a penalty in the Final replay as the Blues lost 3-2 to Spurs. But in 1984, while with Burnley, he was forced to retire because of an arthritic hip, at the age of 26.

This Attleborough schoolboy went on to become one of the most explosive strikers in Division One during his two and a half years in the City first team. A Barnardo boy and an ABA Junior Boxing Finalist, Justin Fashanu made his debut for the Canaries against West Bromwich Albion at the age of 17 in January 1979, and soon established a reputation for making life difficult for the toughest centre-halves. Fashanu scored 40 goals in only 97 senior outings for Norwich before becoming the club's second £1 million departure in the summer of 1981, in what proved a disastrous move to Nottingham Forest. He was never the same threat again at top level, and a combination of serious injury and club-hopping marked his decline. His younger brother, John, sustained a career at the top level for much longer and was capped by England, but Justin, only 15 when this picture was taken, always looked to have more natural ability.

Kevin Reeves quickly blossomed into a polished performer at First Division level and scored eight goals in 21 League games before the end of 1976-77 season. City's most memorable win came on 2 April, when they beat Manchester United 2-1 at Carrow Road. Reeves is shown scoring the Canaries' second goal. The victory was marred by rioting from United followers at the Barclay End of the ground.

Midfielder Colin Suggett, one of the first players to sport the permed look so popular in the late 1970s, in the thick of the action during the 2-1 defeat of Manchester United at Carrow Road in April 1977. Suggett scored City's first goal, one of 29 he scored for the club during a five-year stay. On the floor (7) is United winger Steve Coppell. Looking on (left to right) are Brian Greenhoff, Jimmy Greenhoff, David Jones, Gordon Hill, David McCreery, Martin Peters, Mel Machin and Sammy McIlroy.

Carrow Road was not immune from the plague of hooliganism in the 1970s. The visits of West Ham in 1975 and Manchester United in 1977 brought the worst outbreaks of crowd trouble. There were ugly scenes before and after Manchester United's First Division match at Norwich on 2 April 1977. Here, one United fan receives treatment on the touch-line after supporters spilled on to the pitch to escape trouble on the terraces.

The thin blue line comes under pressure in the Barclay Stand as police and Manchester United fans come face to face during crowd disturbances at Carrow Road. United lost 2-1 – hardly a result which helped the police cause.

Some supporters climbed on to the roof of the Barclay Stand during the riot which followed Manchester United's defeat, and sections of the stand were broken up and used as missiles. In all, there were 30 injured and 19 arrests and the incidents led to much stricter security measures at Norwich for the rest of the 1970s and 1980s. Scenes such as this are, thankfully, rare on English grounds in the 1990s.

Martin Stanford Peters, MBE, one of England's 1966 World Cup winners, brought all his class and experience to the fore in John Bond's bright but brittle team of the late 1970s – not to mention 50 goals in 232 first-team matches. Peters played his last five seasons of First Division football with City before joining Sheffield United as player-coach in 1980 for one unhappy season. Even into his mid-30s, Peters was still being recommended for an England recall as the national team struggled under Don Revie and, to a lesser degree, under Ron Greenwood.

For much of the 1977-78 season, it seemed that Bond's Canaries could be on course to take the club into Europe for the first time. But they ultimately ran out of steam and finished a disappointing 13th. For once, they were above rivals Ipswich Town, who slumped to a perilous 18th – but still managed to steal City's thunder by winning the FA Cup. But Norwich's campaign had its moments and not least in a 3-3 draw against Nottingham Forest on 25 February. Brian Clough's team, who went on to win the championship in their first season after promotion, led 3-0 after only 24 minutes at Carrow Road, but goals from John Ryan, Colin Suggett and debutant Keith Robson represented a storming comeback in front of 26,004 fans. Pictured are goalkeeper Roger Hansbury and defender Tony Powell, up against Forest's Tony Woodcock.

Great goalkeeper that he was, Kevin Keelan had just the occasional rush of blood and was the first goalkeeper to be sent off playing for City, against Northampton in 1965. Here he disputes a controversial goal scored by John Hawley for Leeds in a 2-2 draw at Carrow Road in October 1978. Referee Peter Richardson is unimpressed.

In what proved to be his final season at Carrow Road, goalkeeper Kevin Keelan broke Ron Ashman's long-standing club appearance record. Keelan finished his City career with 673 League and Cup matches to his credit, 11 ahead of Ashman. This picture, from November 1979, shows Keelan receiving a clock to mark his achievement from chairman Sir Arthur South (left) and former chairman Geoffrey Watling.

City began season 1979-80 with a bang and were top of Division One after winning the first three matches. In the League Cup they disposed of Gillingham, Manchester United and West Bromwich Albion to earn a home quarter-final against Liverpool. But that was the end of the Wembley trail as the Merseyside team surged into a three-goal lead, Kevin Reeves reducing the arrears before half-time. It finished 3-1 to Liverpool and there was further disappointment in the FA Cup, where Wolves won 3-2 at Norwich in a fourth-round replay.

Liverpool were back at Carrow Road two months later for one of the most remarkable games ever staged on the ground. A hat-trick by David Fairclough helped them to a 5-3 win over City, but not without their share of trouble. Martin Peters headed Norwich in front with only one minute gone with this typically well-judged effort. Liverpool hit back to lead 2-1, but Kevin Reeves levelled before half-time.

When Fairclough completed his hat-trick in the second half, it looked as if City were beaten, but Justin Fashanu then produced his stunning 'Goal of the Season' to level the match at 3-3. Fashanu's screaming left-foot volley left goalkeeper Ray Clemence clutching at thin air and provided BBC *Match of the Day* with one of its all-time classics.

Now where did that come from? Liverpool goalkeeper Ray Clemence is speechless as City fans in the Main Stand celebrate Fashanu's wonder goal. Clemence needn't have worried, though. His teammates still found time to conjure up two more goals to win 5-3. John Bond, uncharacteristically, blamed son Kevin for the defensive lapses which cost his side the match.

Yugoslavian international midfielder Drazen Muzinic arrived at Carrow Road in September 1980 amid a blaze of publicity as the club's new record signing. But as a parting gift from manager John Bond – who resigned the following month to take over at Manchester City – Muzinic was to prove a costly acquisition at £300,000. City never solved their communication problems with Muzinic and his contract was cancelled after only 23 senior appearances in the summer of 1982. The former Hadjuk Split star is pictured in action for City against Leicester in December 1981, his penultimate match for the club.

The relationship between chairman Sir Arthur South and manager John Bond was one of mutual admiration for most of Bond's seven-year spell as City manager. Sir Arthur once said the club would 'move heaven and earth' to keep Bond, who in turn was always complimentary about Sir Arthur. Only when Bond resigned in October 1980 to become Manchester City manager did the cracks show. The chairman was furious when Bond decided to take John Benson with him to Maine Road as part of his management team – for Sir Arthur had pencilled in Benson as Bond's successor at Carrow Road.

A Kick Up the Eighties

"NEVER a dull moment" is probably the most appropriate way to sum up the seven years in which City were managed by another of the West Ham 'academy', Ken Brown.

Brown, John Bond's assistant for seven years, landed the top job at Carrow Road when he least expected it – for many had wrongly assumed that the two men were inseparable and that Brown would automatically accompany his old colleague to Maine Road.

But, given that he became manager in somewhat bizarre circumstances, there is no denying that Brown was one of the most popular figures ever to take charge of the Canaries.

And there was plenty to keep the supporters on the edge of their seats during his colourful reign. Relegation in 1981, promotion in 1982, FA Youth Cup triumph in 1983, the Milk Cup at Wembley in 1985, followed bitterly by relegation again and expulsion from Europe, then the Second Division championship in 1986 and fifth place in Division One a year later – a bewildering catalogue of triumph and disaster which he negotiated with a smile until his controversial sacking in 1987 with City in another of their unexpected troughs.

Brown, like his predecessor, favoured a broadly attacking game and he too had an easy relationship with the media, albeit with a more diplomatic tongue.

Mel Machin, as chief coach, was regarded as one of the best in the game, and though his partnership with Brown was perhaps not always as harmonious as was publicly portrayed, his tougher image proved a good foil for the benign face of the manager.

Their years in charge brought players of real quality to Norwich, whether it was the experience and international calibre of men such as Mike Channon, Martin O'Neill and David Williams, or the more youthful talent of players like Chris Woods, Dave Watson and Steve Bruce, all destined for greater things with more famous clubs.

Brown and Machin also took City into Europe for the first time – if only the Heysel Stadium disaster had not denied them their UEFA Cup ticket in 1985.

There were days of joy and days of utter despair, among them the FA Cup quarter-final defeat at Brighton in 1983 and the day in 1985 when City were relegated as much by Everton's indifference as by any heroism on the part of Coventry City.

Such was the rollercoaster ride of the Brown era at Carrow Road.

Ken Brown's personal popularity helped see him through some difficult days at Carrow Road as City's fortunes fluctuated greatly in his seven years as manager. They were relegated twice during his reign, yet each time they bounced straight back to Division One. The euphoria which greeted the Milk Cup triumph of 1985 was followed in a matter of weeks by relegation and expulsion from the UEFA Cup because of the withdrawal of English teams after the Heysel disaster. And only six months after City achieved their highest-ever finish in Division One – fifth in 1986-87 – they were second from bottom and Brown was sacked. Throughout it all, he remained a popular figure with the public, who seemed to find the disarming personality more endearing than his outspoken predecessor.

City had a future World Cup star in their squad in 1981-82, but he couldn't even get in the side. New Zealand international Wynton Rufer and his brother Shane played for City Reserves, but despite an impressive trial period, Rufer was unable to play for the first team because of problems over a work permit. Norwich North MP David Ennals (pictured with Rufer) agreed to help, but to no avail. Rufer went on to play in the 1982 World Cup for the Kiwis and became a major success in Europe, notably with Werder Bremen, who won the German Cup, European Cup-winners' Cup and Bundesliga title.

Northern Ireland international Martin O'Neill signed not once but twice for City in the early 1980s, and on both occasions his arrival had a dramatic impact on team fortunes. He first joined the Canaries from Nottingham Forest in February 1981 for £250,000, and his inspirational performances in midfield almost steered the team clear of relegation, until defeat in the last two matches sent them down to Division Two. He moved to Manchester City for a brief and unhappy spell under John Bond in the summer of 1981, but eight months later he was back at Carrow Road to play a crucial role in City's successful promotion push. O'Neill, who skippered Northern Ireland in the 1982 World Cup Finals, had one more First Division season with Norwich before a contract dispute saw him move again in 1983, to Notts County for a tribunal-set fee of £40,000. In June 1995 O'Neill returned once more to Carrow Road, this time as the new Canaries manager, his task to restore Norwich to the Premiership.

This goal from Keith Bertschin sparked scenes of unbridled jubilation among City fans at Hillsborough on the last day of the 1981-82 season. Norwich travelled to Sheffield Wednesday needing a point to clinch promotion, and when Bertschin's goal made it 1-1 with only four minutes left, it seemed the promotion miracle was complete. In one final twist, Wednesday snatched a late winner through Gary Bannister, but as the fans' emotions went through the mincer one more time, Leicester's failure to beat Shrewsbury meant City were up in any case.

The apparent significance of Bertschin's goal prompted his colleagues to indulge in all manner of celebrations, a few minutes prematurely. Martin O'Neill embraces Bertschin on the ground, John Deehan is on his knees giving thanks, and the clenched fist of Dave Watson sums up the mood.

City skipper Mick McGuire looks down on thousands of Canary fans from the balcony at City Hall after his side had clinched promotion to Division One in May 1982. The players were given a rapturous welcome on their open-top bus tour of the city, not least because promotion had seemed so unlikely for much of the campaign. Still in the bottom half of the table in February, City won ten of their last 12 matches to snatch third place.

City had Wembley in their sights when they reached the FA Cup quarter-finals for the first time in 20 years in 1983. They got through to the last eight, courtesy of a 1-0 win over East Anglian rivals Ipswich at Carrow Road in the fifth round, secured by this Keith Bertschin goal. For Bertschin, it was a sweet moment against his old club – not so sweet for goalkeeper Paul Cooper and Town defender Russell Osman (extreme right). A crowd of 28,001 saw the match.

Man of the moment – goalscorer Keith Bertschin battles his way through the crowd at the end of City's fifth-round tie against Ipswich, with Dave Watson (behind) embraced by an ecstatic fan. The quarter-final was an anticlimax, however, with the Canaries beaten 1-0 at Brighton by a controversial Jimmy Case goal.

Dave Stringer returned to Carrow Road in 1980 to take charge of the City youth team and in 1982-83, his youngsters did the double, winning the South East Counties League and the FA Youth Cup. The Youth Cup win, in particular, caught the imagination of supporters as the Canaries beat Southend, Arsenal, Watford, Manchester United, Luton and Everton to lift the trophy for the first time. Three of Stringer's squad made a sustained impact at first-team level. Louie Donowa was a member of the Milk Cup-winning side of 1985; Tony Spearing played 80 senior games at left-back before moving to Leicester, Plymouth and Peterborough; and Jeremy Goss was still at Carrow Road 12 years on, having been a UEFA Cup star and had a testimonial. Back row (left to right): Dave Stringer, Brendan McIntyre, Mark Crowe, Jon Rigby, John Waddell, Paul Clayton, Daryl Godbold, Harvey Simpson, Matthew Spillman. Front row: Tony Spearing, Jeremy Goss, Neil Riley, Austin O'Connor, Andrew Pearce, Paul Kinnaird, Louie Donowa, Mark Metcalf.

The arrival of Mike Channon at Carrow Road in December 1982 at the age of 34 did not, at the time, seem likely to be more than a stopgap measure as City sought to consolidate their place in Division One. But, after a free transfer from Bristol Rovers, Channon stayed for two and a half years and was still able to deliver the goods on a stage as grand as Wembley at the age of 36. He scored 25 goals in 108 games for the Canaries and his enduring skill and infectious enthusiasm made him immensely popular with supporters. Channon, who won 46 England caps, still conjured up moments of pure genius long after his international days were over. He moved to Portsmouth in the summer of 1985 and is now a successful racehorse trainer.

Dave Bennett was one of the most gifted players to grace Carrow Road in the 1980s, but his career was cut short by a succession of injuries. He was a key member of City's promotion team in 1982 and the following season, proved he could live with the best in Division One with some classy displays as a left-sided midfielder. In 1984, however, he was forced to quit top-class football and was the first player to benefit from the private accident insurance scheme introduced by the Professional Footballers' Association. Bennett played 77 times for the Canaries, scoring 11 goals.

This goal provided City supporters with probably their most enjoyable memory from the 1980s – reaching Wembley and beating Ipswich Town to do it. Steve Bruce, right hand aloft, turns away after heading home Mark Barham's corner to give the Canaries a 2-0 win in the second leg of their 1985 Milk Cup semi-final against Town, securing a 2-1 aggregate triumph. Bruce's winner came only two minutes from time. Teammates (left to right) Louie Donowa, Mike Channon and John Deehan show their delight, while the bewildered Ipswich quartet are Trevor Putney, goalkeeper Paul Cooper, George Burley and Terry Butcher.

The goal which secured the Milk Cup for City and gave their fans a Wembley win to celebrate at the third attempt. Asa Hartford is embraced by Mark Barham and Dennis Van Wyk after Hartford's shot had flown in via the chest of Sunderland defender Gordon Chisholm. The goal came at the start of the second half, but there was one shock in store before the Canaries got their hands on the silverware.

Jubilation on the bench at Wembley as City go ahead against Sunderland. Brown and Machin (back to camera) lead the Canary contingent's celebrations, along with Dale Gordon, physiotherapist Tim Sheppard and substitute John Devine. Gary Rowell, the former Sunderland player who was part of City's squad, is more reserved about it all.

Sunderland were given the chance to get on terms only three minutes after Hartford's goal when Dennis Van Wyk handled and referee Neil Midgley pointed to the spot. But up stepped Clive Walker – who promptly fired wide, his shot just clipping the outside of the post on its way. He became the first player to miss a penalty in a Wembley Final.

Skipper Dave Watson was 23 when he led City to victory at Wembley, and had already been captain for two years. He shouldered the responsibility superbly and quickly gained international recognition, making his England debut in the summer of 1984 in a 2-0 win over Brazil in Rio de Janeiro. He won six caps during his time with the Canaries, but his omission from the World Cup squad in 1986 was a major disappointment. Watson moved to Everton in August 1986 for £1 million and won a further six caps over the next two seasons. He was back in the Royal Box to collect the FA Cup for Everton in 1995.

The familiar Wembley celebration scene, but unfamiliar colours as Norwich City display the Milk Cup. Back row (left to right): Mel Machin (chief coach), Louie Donowa, Steve Bruce, Chris Woods, Dave Watson, John Deehan, John Devine. Front row: Mark Barham, Peter Mendham, Paul Haylock, Mike Channon, Dennis Van Wyk, Asa Hartford.

One moment every Norwich City fan had waited for – their team doing a lap of honour at Wembley with a major trophy. Goalkeeper Chris Woods and skipper Dave Watson carry off the Milk Cup, Louie Donowa flies the flag and substitute John Devine examines his medal. Little did they imagine that City would be relegated two months later.

The highlight of the Brown-Machin partnership was the Milk Cup Final victory over Sunderland at Wembley, and the manager and chief coach joined in a joyful lap of honour. Machin's tough character but also innovative approach as coach, won him many admirers and made him the ideal foil for Brown. Mike Channon described Machin as the best coach he had worked with.

John Deehan, with a firm grip on the Milk Cup after City's Wembley win, was one of the most successful goalscorers in club history. His 70 goals in 199 appearances between 1981 and 1986 put him fifth in the all-time list and it was

something of a surprise when he was swapped for Ipswich midfielder Trevor Putney as the Canaries returned to Division One. "I didn't expect to be used as bait," he said at the time. After spells at Manchester City and Barnsley, where he combined playing with his role as assistant manager, he returned to Norwich in 1992 as assistant manager to Mike Walker.

Asa Hartford had only seven months as a Norwich City player, but secured a unique place in club history as the only man to score for them at Wembley – few worried that his 1985 Milk Cup winner took a big deflection off Gordon Chisholm. Hartford, who won 50 international caps for Scotland, had a tenacious approach in midfield which sometimes made him unpopular with opposing fans, but he gave the Canaries added bite during his 40 first-team matches, which yielded five goals. Hartford hit the soccer headlines in 1971 when, at the age of 21, his proposed £175,000 move from West Bromwich to Leeds fell through because he was diagnosed as having a hole in the heart. But he played at top level for a further 14 years and has since had a string of coaching and managerial posts.

Sir Arthur South's 12-year stint as Norwich City chairman ended in 1985, following disagreements at boardroom level over the building of the new City Stand at Carrow Road to replace the Main Stand badly damaged by fire the previous year. The entire board resigned on 25 November and after a caretaker period, a new board was elected with Robert Chase as chairman and Jimmy Jones vice-chairman. Sir Arthur had had his critics, like all football club chairmen, but few doubted that he had the interests of the club at heart – right back to 1957, when he spearheaded the appeal which saved City from extinction.

Champions! The Canaries display their Canon League Division Two trophy after the final home match of 1985-86, when they beat Leeds United 4-0 at Carrow Road. So convincingly did City take the title that they were champions with three games to spare, and finished 11 points clear of the fourth placed side, Portsmouth. Back row (left to right): Dale Gordon, David Williams, Paul Clayton, Mike Phelan, Chris Woods, Steve Bruce, Ian Culverhouse, Garry Brooke. Front row: Dennis Van Wyk, Dave Watson, John Deehan, Kevin Drinkell.

Kevin Drinkell became the fourth man to win City's Player of the Year award twice, his goalscoring feats putting him top of the poll in 1986 and 1987. Drinkell joined City from Grimsby for a tribunal set fee of £105,000 and went on to score 57 times in 150 first-team games in his three seasons at Carrow Road. He had a remarkable fitness record, missing very few games for City. Drinkell here signs a new contract in February 1987, with Mel Machin (left) and Ken Brown looking on. But little more than a year later, all three had parted company with City, Drinkell the last to leave in a £500,000 move to Glasgow Rangers in the summer of 1988.

Below: The date is 9 November 1987, and they're getting that Monday morning feeling. A grimfaced Ken Brown has to sit and listen while City chairman Robert Chase explains to reporters why Brown has been sacked. A dismal start to the 1987-88 season left City in a perilous position near the foot of Division One, but Brown's dismissal was still met with a wave of protest and led to an extraordinary general meeting two months later. Chase and his fellow directors survived and Dave Stringer stepped in as manager to steer the Canaries to safety. For Brown, it was a sad end to 14 years at Carrow Road, seven of them as John Bond's assistant and the next seven as manager. His son, Kenny, was a first-team player at the time but left the club at the end of the season, moving to Plymouth – Brown's next base as manager – then West Ham.

Right: There is no easy way to sack a manager but Ken Brown's removal from the job at Carrow Road prompted a wave of public sympathy. Fans were desperate for a reversal of the downward trend which took City rapidly into a relegation battle, but at the same time, most of them would have liked Brown to be offered some kind of upstairs role at the club in recognition of his 14 years' service. "I used to say West Ham was my club, but now I regard Norwich as my club," Brown told reporters on the day he was dismissed. He was later caretaker manager of Shrewsbury (for two weeks), managed Plymouth, and in 1994 he was recruited by Terry Venables as an England scout.

Dreams of the Double

MESSRS Owen and Steel were not the only two Davids to form what they hoped would be a winning alliance in 1987.

With the sacking of Ken Brown in November 1987, control of the City first-team passed into the hands of his two deputies.

Dave Stringer and David Williams were given one simple instruction – to save the Canaries from relegation to Division Two.

This they achieved with such aplomb that City even climbed into the top half of Division One at one point in the spring of 1988, and a final position of 14th was more than satisfactory given their plight just before Christmas.

Yet few would have expected the same squad, with only one or two additions, to provide a sustained challenge for the championship in 1988-89, the bookies making them 150-1 for the title.

City went even further than that, though, and in reaching their first FA Cup semi-final for 30 years, there was even hope of doing the League and Cup double, a scenario most would have put down as pure fantasy little more than a year before.

Norwich, quite simply, were the best side in the country for the first half of 1988-89 and it was not until April, when they suffered three successive Division One defeats and exit from the FA Cup at the hands of Everton, that the bubble finally burst.

Nonetheless, fourth place was City's best-ever finish in the League and the fact that they failed to build on such a good platform in the next three seasons under Stringer was due as much to the undermining of the squad by the constant sale of the best players as it was to any shortcomings on the part of the management team.

The FA Cup still offered the Canaries a possible route to Europe, however, and they might have done better in both 1991 and 1992. In the first instance, Nottingham Forest won a drab quarter-final 1-0 at Carrow Road. In the second, City performed dismally in capitulating to Sunderland by the same score in a Hillsborough semi-final.

That defeat triggered a marked decline in form in the final weeks of Stringer's stewardship, and with top-flight status only narrowly preserved, he opted to resign from what had become a difficult job.

Williams was not offered the post and so he, too, moved on, but they had certainly played their part in enhancing the reputation of the Canaries after taking over in such hazardous circumstances four and a half years earlier.

Dave Stringer was promoted from reserve-team manager to assistant manager when Mel Machin quit Carrow Road in the summer of 1987, but could not have expected further promotion so soon. Ken Brown was dismissed on 9 November and Stringer appointed acting manager. The job was made permanent after Christmas victories over Derby and Chelsea lifted the gloom over Carrow Road. It was the start of an 11-match period which brought City seven wins and three draws and banished fears of relegation.

David Williams had a relatively brief playing career with City, but was a key contributor in midfield as they won the Second Division championship and re-established themselves in Division One. His polished displays made one wonder why he had spent the rest of his career in the lower divisions with Bristol Rovers. An Achilles injury restricted his appearances in the top flight, but when Mel Machin left Norwich, Williams' previous experience as Rovers player-manager and his astute reading of the game made him a natural choice as player-coach. Williams, who represented Wales at every level, was promoted to assistant manager at Carrow Road in 1988 and did the job for four seasons before moving to coaching posts with Bournemouth, then Everton.

John O'Neill goes down as arguably the most unlucky player in City's history, for after joining the club as a replacement for the departed Steve Bruce in December 1987, his Canary career lasted only 34 minutes. Following a collision with Wimbledon's John Fashanu during his City debut at Plough Lane, O'Neill was stretchered off with ruptured knee ligaments and forced to retire from the game, having played his last match at the age of 29. Arriving in the same week as Robert Fleck, O'Neill was Dave Stringer's first signing, at £100,000 from Queen's Park Rangers. Gary Lineker was the star attraction at O'Neill's testimonial at Carrow Road in May 1989.

Andy Townsend's signing at £300,000 from Southampton in the summer of 1988 proved a master-stroke by the Canaries as the left-sided midfielder exploded on to the scene. His first goal for the club was a spectacular late winner in a 2-1 victory at Manchester United in October as City opened up a six-point gap at the top of the table. So big an impression did Townsend create that he was recruited by Republic of Ireland manager Jack Charlton before the end of the season and went on to play for his adopted country in the World Cup Finals in Italy in 1990 and the USA in 1994. After 88 senior games for City, however, Townsend took up the option of leaving a year before the end of his contract and moved to Chelsea in the summer of 1990, saying he needed 'a bigger stage' on which to perform.

City's flying start to 1988-89 caught many of the First Division's big spenders by surprise, none more so than Tottenham, who came to Carrow Road in October parading summer signings Paul Gascoigne and Paul Stewart. Spurs were on the receiving end of a 3-1 defeat, and the Canaries followed it up four days later with a 2-1 win against Manchester United at Old Trafford. Here, Dale Gordon accelerates away from Stewart during the win over Spurs.

Alan Taylor's appearance in the City first team in November 1988 represented one of the most extraordinary comebacks in Football League history, for his introduction as a substitute against Sheffield Wednesday – pictured here against Mel Sterland and Chris Turner – came eight years and seven months after his previous match for Norwich. Taylor asked to train with City at the start of the 1988-89 season after moving back to Norfolk, looked so sharp that he played for the reserves, and then won a first-team call-up. He even scored in a 1-1 draw at Queen's Park Rangers on 2 January 1989. Taylor had originally joined City in 1979 for £90,000 from West Ham, for whom he scored both goals in the 1975 FA Cup Final. But his first stay at Carrow Road lasted only a year before he moved to Canada for four seasons.

City's neck-and-neck battle with Arsenal at the top of Division One was not the only thing to fire the imagination of the fans. The tantalising possibility of a League and FA Cup double was also opening up as the Canaries reached the quarter-finals for the first time in six years. After beating Port Vale and non-League Sutton United in the opening two rounds, they reached the last eight with a thrilling 3-2 win over Sheffield United in the fifth round at Carrow Road. The Third Division leaders made City fight all the way, though, in front of 24,139 fans. Here Andy Townsend fights for possession with United's Mark Todd.

City advanced to the semi-finals with a 3-1 win over West Ham in their quarter-final replay at Carrow Road, following a 0-0 draw at Upton Park. Hero of the night was Malcolm Allen, who scored twice in the first half as a crowd of 25,785 witnessed a thrilling night's action. Allen (9) is pictured turning away after scoring his second goal, with striking partner Robert Rosario leaping in delight. The dejected West Ham defenders are Tony Gale (4) and Gary Strodder.

Arms aloft in celebration is winger Dale Gordon after scoring the third goal in City's 3-1 FA Cup quarter-final replay win over West Ham. Gordon was the club's Player of the Year in 1988-89 and made a total of 261 appearances for the Canaries, scoring 43 goals, before joining Glasgow Rangers in 1991 for £1.2 million. Gordon, from Caister-on-Sea in Norfolk, played for England Schoolboys at Wembley at the age of 14. From Ibrox he moved to West Ham for £750,000 in 1993.

Below: The goal which ended City's hopes of a first-ever FA Cup Final appearance: Everton winger Pat Nevin nudges the ball over the line to give his side a 1-0 victory at Villa Park in what was destined to be forever regarded as the most forgotten semi-final in the history of the competition. The date was 15 April 1989, and 80 miles away at Sheffield, 95 supporters lost their lives in the Hillsborough disaster at the Liverpool-Nottingham Forest tie. Everton's delight at victory and City's dejection in defeat were forgotten when set against a tragedy which stunned the nation. For the record, the City players pictured are (left to right) Andy Linighan, goalkeeper Bryan Gunn, Ian Butterworth, Ian Crook and Mark Bowen. Everton's Tony Cottee and Kevin Sheedy are the men poised to celebrate.

City had their chances against Everton, notably in the first half at Villa Park. Here Andy Linighan (right) gets in a header in spite of the attentions of Pat Van den Hauwe and Dave Watson, with Kevin Sheedy, Neville Southall and Kevin Ratcliffe also watching, and City's Malcolm Allen (8) waiting to pounce.

City had reached the semi-final in style, scoring 17 goals in the first four rounds, but they were hit by a series of major set-backs in the last two weeks before the match against Everton. The loss of three successive League games in eight days put an end to their championship dream, and in the third defeat at Coventry, they lost skipper Michael Phelan with a hamstring injury. Then, on the eve of the semi-final, striker Robert Fleck had to withdraw because of the sudden death of his father. Defeat is a matter of minutes away as Phelan (extreme left) looks on from the bench at Villa Park, with (left to right) physiotherapist Tim Sheppard, Dave Stringer, David Williams and Malcolm Allen looking suitably anxious.

The end of City's semi-final against Everton and (left to right) Robert Rosario, Ian Crook and Trevor Putney leave the field, with goalkeeper Bryan Gunn applauding the fans, some 19,000 of whom went to Villa Park in the hope of seeing their side reach Wembley.

City's eventual position of fourth in Division One in 1988-89 was a disappointment as they had hardly been out of the top two all season, but it was still their highest-ever League placing and a good deal better than anyone dared hope nine months earlier. And they began the next season as if they were about to repeat or even better that achievement, going unbeaten for the first nine matches, including a 2-2 draw at home to Tottenham. Mark Bowen celebrates his second-half equaliser with the help of Andy Linighan (centre) and Robert Rosario. It was the first of seven League goals that season for full-back Bowen, whose outstanding form earned him the Player of the Year award.

Bowen struck again a week after the Tottenham match when he scored the winner at Millwall. City's 1-0 victory at The Den made them the first side since Leeds United in 1970 to start their First Division programme with four clean sheets away from home. Bowen, seen arms aloft after his goal at Millwall with Dale Gordon in pursuit, had also scored in the Canaries' 3-2 win on the same ground the season before.

As City's profile rose through their progress under Dave Stringer, so the profile of chairman Robert Chase became higher, too. He and his directors survived the storm which followed Ken Brown's dismissal, and as Stringer and David Williams effected a transformation in the Canaries' form, so the pressure eased, at least temporarily. Chase and Jimmy Jones (left) became directors in 1983 and were elected as chairman and vice-chairman after the entire board resigned in 1985. They had little to cheer about when this picture was taken, though, during a 4-1 defeat at Luton in October 1989.

Mud, glorious mud played a significant part in City's FA Cup third-round tie at Exeter on 6 January 1990, an enthralling battle worthy of a grander stage. The Fourth Division leaders matched the Canaries stride for stride in appalling conditions and looked set for a shock win when Darren Rowbotham headed them in front after 85 minutes. But Robert Fleck came to City's rescue with the equaliser straight from the kick-off. Fleck came close to losing his shirt in the celebrations which followed. Behind him, Robert Rosario shows his delight. City won the replay 2-0 but went out of the competition in a fourth-round replay at Liverpool, beaten 3-1.

The lean and hungry look belongs to the future £5 million striker, Chris Sutton, in action as a 17-year-old for City Youth against Queen's Park Rangers in April 1990. And the silver-haired spectator in the background at Trowse is none other than Mike Walker, reserve-team boss at the time. Walker and Sutton became central figures in City's challenge for the Premier League title and their entry into the UEFA Cup three years later. Few would have imagined on this sunny spring day that their eventual departures from Carrow Road, coming within six months of each other, would cause such a storm.

City began to glimpse the twin towers of Wembley again in 1991 after a brilliant FA Cup fifth-round victory over holders Manchester United at Carrow Road. Robert Fleck, pictured in celebratory mood with one of the ball-boys after the match, scored the opening goal in the Canaries' 2-1 win. Brian McClair put United level, but Dale Gordon struck for City's second-half winner. The result earned a home tie against Nottingham Forest in the quarter-finals, but a goal from Roy Keane ended another FA Cup dream.

Ian Culverhouse proved an outstanding buy when City snapped him up from Tottenham in October 1985 for a mere £50,000. For the next nine years, he was a model of consistency in the defence, playing mostly at right-back but at times in a highly effective sweeper role, most notably during City's UEFA Cup campaign. Culverhouse was voted Player of the Year in 1990-91 and went on to make a total of 369 appearances for the club, moving into the top ten in club history. His departure from Carrow Road after failing to agree terms in the summer of 1994 was a major disappointment for the fans and a sad way to sever his City connection. Neither did it help, as the Canaries went spinning towards relegation, to know that Culverhouse was experiencing the same trauma at his new club, Swindon.

Stringer's Canaries looked as if they would finally make it to an FA Cup Final in 1992 when they reached their second semi-final in four seasons. After victories over Barnsley and Millwall, they easily accounted for Notts County in the fifth round, winning 3-0 at Carrow Road to reach the last eight. Chris Sutton (right) embraces Robert Fleck (centre) and Rob Newman after giving Norwich an early lead against County. Both Newman and Sutton were on target in the quarter-final as City beat Southampton 2-1 in a tempestuous replay. The Saints had two players sent off.

Chris Sutton's emergence as a regular first-team player at the age of 18 provided one of the bright spots of Stringer's final season as manager. But at this stage, it was unclear whether Sutton would settle down as a centre-half or striker. He played in both roles in his first two seasons of first-team football as both Stringer and Mike Walker pondered the best option. However, it was Sutton's goals which helped City into the FA Cup semi-finals in 1992. Here he brushes up his skills with his father, Mike, a teammate of Stringer with the Canaries in the 1960s. Sutton senior also played for Chester and Carlisle.

No, it's not an audition for *Dr Who* or *Star Trek*. But City's quarter-final victory over Southampton was not without its casualties. Robert Fleck suffered two cracked ribs and faced a long battle to be fit for the semi-final against Sunderland at Hillsborough. City hired the latest technology in a desperate bid to get their star striker fit. The hyperbaric oxygen machine was designed for quick healing, and Fleck did indeed line up against Sunderland. But there was no happy ending.

Further injuries to David Phillips and Ian Crook, plus suspension for striker Darren Beckford, limited City's options severely for the semi-final against Sunderland, but they should still have been capable of disposing of modest Second Division opponents. Instead, another disappointing semi-final display ended in another 1-0 defeat as John Byrne's 33rd-minute goal took the Wearsiders to Wembley. Sutton and skipper Mark Bowen had their chances for Norwich, but the defeat at Hillsborough could also have been heavier. Goalkeeper Mark Walton and Rob Newman scramble the ball off the line during a late Sunderland attack, with Colin Woodthorpe on the floor.

City's FA Cup exit coincided with an alarming slump in form in Division One and by the time Wimbledon came to Carrow Road for the final home match of 1991-92, a point was still needed to avoid relegation. A goal from Fleck in a 1-1 draw was just enough, but the Canaries' near-fatal slide down the table heralded the end of Dave Stringer's reign as manager. It had been a stressful season with its highs and lows – City also reached the Rumbelows Cup quarter-finals – and Stringer announced his resignation the day before the final League fixture at Leeds, leaving David Williams and Mike Walker in temporary charge of the side.

The Road to Europe

A MONTH of fevered speculation over who would succeed Dave Stringer as City manager was brought to an end in near farcical circumstances on 1 June 1992.

It seemed almost certain that Phil Neal, the former Liverpool and England full-back and one-time Bolton manager, would be appointed in Stringer's place after a favourable interview at Carrow Road.

But on the eve of the scheduled announcement, Neal was declared out of the running after the club claimed he was unwilling to move to Norwich. The point was hotly contested but amid claim and counter-claim, Mike Walker stepped into the manager's office, promoted from reserve-team boss, with former City striker John Deehan as his assistant.

The manner of Walker's appointment was hardly flattering, but if it bothered him, he certainly didn't let it show. Instead, the collapse of negotiations with Neal proved one of the greatest strokes of good fortune City had ever experienced.

Walker and Deehan were to take the Canaries higher than ever before over the next 18 months, and City's equally rapid descent from such heights will forever be a matter of bitter regret for the thousands of fans who delighted in their team's new-found fame.

The Canaries booked their European ticket by finishing third in the new FA Premier League in 1992-93 and claiming the UEFA Cup place made available by Arsenal when they won both domestic Cup competitions.

Yet for much of that memorable season, it seemed Walker's men might complete mission impossible and finish the campaign as champions. They started with a bang and despite a 7-1 humbling at the hands of Blackburn in October, City had built up an eight-point lead by early December.

They sustained that challenge until early April, when Manchester United won 3-1 at Carrow Road to grasp the initiative and march on to the title for the first time in 26 years.

But Europe beckoned as the Canaries' consolation prize and how gloriously they grasped the opportunity. Victories over Vitesse Arnhem and giants Bayern Munich – including a 2-1 first-leg victory in the Olympic Stadium – gave Walker and his players national celebrity status, and the heroic nature of their third-round defeat by Internazionale made sure there was little to diminish the glow.

City had become heroes again, not just in their own back yard, but as the darlings of the BBC and national media. Their arrival as a team to be reckoned with beyond their own shores should have marked just the end of the beginning, but defeat in Milan was in fact the beginning of the end for Walker, Deehan and for City themselves.

In the four weeks which followed Dave Stringer's departure from the manager's office, City were reported to have drawn up a short list from which they would pick his replacement. Martin O'Neill, Bryan Robson and even Ivan Golac were among those mentioned in connection with the job, but former Bolton boss Phil Neal emerged as favourite. He was even photographed with the chairman and vice-chairman in 'welcome to Carrow Road' pose. However, a last-minute hitch put Neal out of the running and on 1 June, Mike Walker was appointed manager, with John Deehan, the former City striker, brought in from Barnsley as his number two. Walker, reserve-team boss, had made no secret of his desire to move up, and it brought dramatic results from the word go.

Right: One of Mike Walker's first moves as manager was to reappoint central defender Ian Butterworth as captain. Butterworth had been given the skipper's role by Dave Stringer in 1989, but lost the job in 1991 after he complained about being left out for the FA Cup quarter-final against his old club, Nottingham Forest. Mark Bowen took over from Butterworth, but Walker plumped for Butterworth to lead his team into the new season. The unflappable centre-back had eight seasons at Carrow Road, but in the summer of 1994, a freak water sports accident left him with serious knee damage and he announced his retirement, at the age of 31, in May 1995, after 293 first-team games for the club. For the former England Under-21 international, and for City, it was a sad day.

Far right: The signing of Mark Robins from Manchester United for £800,000 on the eve of the new season was the perfect answer to fans lamenting the £2.1 million departure of Robert Fleck to Chelsea. Robins started City's opening match at Arsenal on the bench, but introduced on the hour at Highbury, he scored with his third touch of the ball and added a second as the Canaries transformed a 2-0 deficit into a 4-2 win. He then quickly found favour with his new home crowd by scoring in the 2-1 win over Chelsea four days later. A new hero had arrived – and one who was not afraid to stand up to Chelsea iron man Vinny Jones. Fleck, under the terms of his transfer, was not allowed to play at Norwich that night.

The unstoppable Robins was on target again, scoring twice as City completed an early season double with a 3-2 win over Chelsea at Stamford Bridge after being two goals down. They were assisted, it must be said, by some eccentric goalkeeping by Dave Beasant, but they were top of the table on merit. Walker's other pre-season capture, Gary Megson, is also in picture. His arrival on a free transfer from Manchester City added new aggression to the midfield department, although at 33 he was seen as a short-term replacement.

Goalkeeper Bryan Gunn earned the admiration of City fans everywhere for his courage in the face of family tragedy following the death of his two-year-old daughter, Francesca, in October 1992, from leukaemia. He missed one match before returning to action against Queen's Park Rangers at Carrow Road, where he was given a tremendous reception. Francesca's death led to the launching of the Bryan Gunn Appeal, which raised well over £300,000 by mid-1995 for research into childhood leukaemia. Bryan and his wife, Susan, and their younger daughter Melissa gave their wholehearted support to an ever-growing list of fund-raising functions.

Mark Robins' popularity with the fans hit new heights in November when he scored a hat-trick in City's 3-2 win at Oldham in a match switched to Monday night for a Sky TV screening, as part of the new Premier League deal with the satellite company. Many of City's most loyal fans were flown to the match for the same cost as the normal coach trip, and had the added bonus of travelling home with the team. Here, Robins heads the opening goal, and though Oldham twice fought level, he had a last-minute winner up his sleeve for City.

A vital goal for the Canaries – and the wave from David Phillips after his successful penalty kick proved to be one of farewell. The goal gave City a 1-0 victory over Liverpool in their final home match of the 1992-93 season, and proved crucial in helping to secure third place in the Premier League and passage into the UEFA Cup the following season. But Phillips was to play no part in the Canaries' European campaign, rejecting a new contract in the close

City maintained their title challenge to the closing weeks of the season, when the championship became a three-horse race between themselves, Aston Villa and Manchester United. Villa were the leaders when they came to Carrow Road on 24 March for what proved to be a gripping night's entertainment, settled by a winner from John Polston nine minutes from time. The goal put City back on top of the Premier League. This was typical of a night of frantic goalmouth action – Villa trio Earl Barrett (2) goalkeeper Mark Bosnich (on ground) and Paul McGrath trying to scramble the ball away from City's Mark Robins and David Phillips (11). The Canaries' win set up another title showdown against Manchester United at Norwich 12 days later, but this time it was United's night as three early goals put the match beyond City's reach and triggered a relentless charge towards the title for the Old Trafford club.

season and moving to Nottingham Forest for a fee set by tribunal. Incidentally, the penalty came about in bizarre circumstances. Liverpool goalkeeper David James kicked out at John Polston following a City corner and was shown the red card. The referee also pointed to the spot, and substitute 'keeper Mike Hooper's first touch was in picking the ball out of the net.

The 1993-94 season was a memorable one for Jeremy Goss in more ways than one. It was not only his testimonial year, but it was a season in which he hit the headlines with a series of explosive goals in key matches. Here is the first of them, a stunning volley in the 4-0 win at Leeds in August 1993 which earned him the BBC Goal of the Month award. He also scored the winner in the local derby against Ipswich at Carrow Road, scored in both legs of the UEFA Cup victory over Bayern Munich, and became the last player to score in front of the famous Kop terrace at Anfield as City beat Liverpool 1-0 in their final away match of the campaign. Coincidentally, the Leeds defender wearing number 16 is none other than Jon Newsome, who became the Canaries' first £1 million signing in the summer of 1994.

Jon Newsome seeks a temporary loan of Efan Ekoku's shorts during the Canaries' 4-0 win at Leeds. Ekoku made only a brief appearance as substitute at Elland Road and did not get on the scoresheet, but was saving his goals up for the trip to Goodison Park the following month, where he scored four times in a 5-1 win over Everton, the first City player to do so in a League match since Tom Johnston at Shrewsbury in 1952.

Take your partner – this little dance between Ruel Fox and Mark Robins at Elland Road was among the more elaborate forms of celebration which crept into the game in the 1990s as players sought more imaginative ways to share their delight with the fans. Backward somersaults, synchronised diving, Aylesbury's famous duck walk and even shirt stripping became popular before the FA stepped in on the grounds of taste.

City's entry into Europe in 1993 was marked by a stunning 3-0 success over Dutch seeds Vitesse Arnhem in the UEFA Cup first round, first leg at Carrow Road. Though the Canaries took half an hour to find their feet as the Dutch set off at a blistering pace, they moved into top gear in the second half and goals followed from Efan Ekoku, Jeremy Goss and John Polston. The Dutch had clearly underestimated the European new boys, and it is remarkable now to think that only 16,818 were there to see it. Polston is shown celebrating his crucial third goal, with Ekoku and Chris Sutton equally jubilant.

For years, City fans had dreamed of seeing their team's name in lights at venues such as the Olympic Stadium – and the dream came true during the Canaries' memorable UEFA Cup run. Their victory over Vitesse Arnhem earned them a second-round tie against Bayern Munich, with the first leg in Germany on 19 October on what was destined to be probably the greatest night in City's history.

The most abiding image of City's UEFA Cup run was this picture of Jeremy Goss volleying them into the lead against Bayern Munich 12 minutes into the first leg of their second-round tie. The goal was replayed time and again as TV trailers helped plug live coverage of the second leg. A header from Mark Bowen made it 2-0 to City after 31 minutes, and though Christian Nerlinger headed a goal for Bayern before half-time, some stout defending and one magnificent save by Bryan Gunn from Adolfo Valencia enabled City to hang on to their 2-1 lead.

They became one of the best-known double acts in Europe in the autumn of 1993 – Mike Walker and Jeremy Goss, here celebrating after victory over Bayern Munich in the Olympic Stadium. Walker had been City's reserve-team boss for four and a half years before succeeding Dave Stringer, and Goss spent much of his time in that reserve side. To see both men in the European spotlight was somehow fitting as the Canaries shook off their backwoods label once and for all – or so it seemed at the time.

Welcome home – City's Welsh international duo, Jeremy Goss and Mark Bowen, fly the flag at Norwich Airport on their return from Munich, where their goals secured an historic win.

The Jeremy Goss fan club were out in force for the second leg against Bayern Munich at Carrow Road, even to the point of donning yellow and green curly wigs and spelling out his name for all the world to see. Their hero didn't let them down, either.

A goal from Colombian striker Adolfo Valencia brought Bayern level on aggregate after only five minutes of the second leg and made it a nervous night for a crowd of 20,829. If the score remained the same, City would still go through on away goals, but Goss went one better than that. Five minutes into the second half, he volleyed home from close range after Chris Sutton had flicked on a cross from Mark Bowen. Here, Goss sets off in celebration with Darren Eadie close behind.

City's encounter with one of European soccer's biggest names seemed to bring the best out of each and every member of the side. Rob Newman was outstanding in defence, and this from a player who had been asked to play in midfield when he first joined the Canaries, and also in attack. Here Newman is in hot pursuit of Dutch midfielder Jan Wouters.

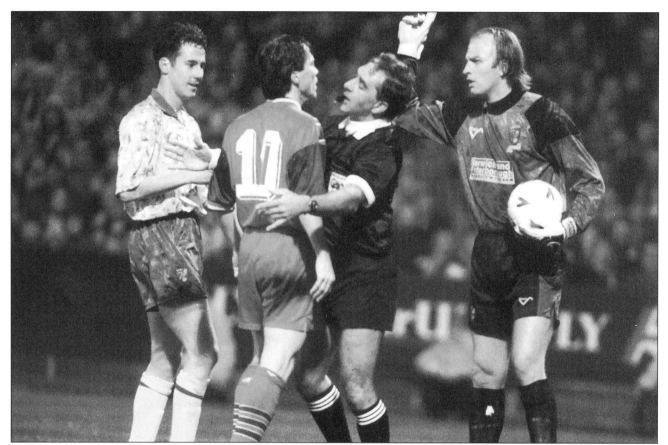

Defeat at the hands of England's European new boys was difficult to take for Lothar Matthäus, Bayern's German international captain, and tempers became frayed towards the end of the second leg. Referee Vandenwijngaert had to step in after this difference of opinion between Matthäus and City goalkeeper Bryan Gunn, with Ian Culverhouse (left) in the role of peacemaker.

It's all over – and the magnitude of City's achievement in knocking out Bayern begins to sink in. Chris Sutton raises his arms to the crowd, while behind him his teammates savour a moment they will remember for the rest of their careers.

It's that man again. Goss, who performed a lap of honour after swapping shirts with Matthäus, joins up with manager Walker to take the acclaim of a full house at Carrow Road. It was a purple patch for Goss, who scored again three days later as City won 2-1 at Sheffield United on their return to Premiership action.

City's victory over Bayern brought them a third-round tie against another of Europe's crack outfits in Internazionale. At a frosty Carrow Road on 24 November – the game was given the go-ahead after a morning inspection – the two sides fought out a tense battle. Chris Sutton finds himself outnumbered two to one by Massimo Paganin (left) and Guiseppe Bergomi, the Milan skipper.

The goal which wrecked City's European dream came ten minutes from the end of the first leg against Internazionale. Rob Newman tripped Ruben Sosa and Dennis Bergkamp scored from the penalty spot. Bergkamp, seen here celebrating his successful spot-kick, also scored the only goal in the second leg, but his goal in Milan came so late as to be academic. It was victory at Norwich which did the real damage.

Striker Efan Ekoku returned after a 12-match absence through injury for City's second leg against Internazionale. It was a gamble by Mike Walker, whose team was ravaged by injuries and suspension, but the Canaries made light of their problems and dominated the match. Ekoku's pace unsettled the Italians, especially in the first half, when both he and Sutton came agonisingly close to levelling the tie. It was rough justice on City when Bergkamp scored two minutes from time to give Inter a 2-0 aggregate win, but the goal did not detract from an heroic display which had Canary fans singing long after the final whistle.

Decline and Fall

FEW who stood and cheered the Canaries in the Olympic Stadium in Munich or the San Siro Stadium in Milan in the autumn of 1993 would have believed it possible that, little more than 18 months later, they and their team would have to face up to life in the Endsleigh League.

But the seeds of City's self-destruction were sown before they had even touched down from Milan, with manager Mike Walker's plea to club chairman Robert Chase to 'open the purse strings' triggering a sequence of events which were destined to drag the club into a frightening downward spiral over the next year and a half.

Just 30 days after basking in the adulation of Canary fans in Italy, Walker resigned to become manager of struggling Everton, clear in his own mind that there was to be no major change of policy at Carrow Road and eager to test out his managerial acumen at a better-known club.

Like many of his predecessors, John Deehan landed the City manager's job at extremely short notice, but there was initial optimism about his chances of keeping up the good work. He had, after all, played a key part in the team's European success and it was felt that continuity was essential in such an uncertain atmosphere.

Within a matter of weeks, however, supporters were given the first hint that City were set to abandon the ambition which had taken them so far in so short a space of time.

Walker no sooner had his feet under his desk at Goodison Park than he was followed out of Carrow Road by star forward Ruel Fox, sold to Newcastle for £2.25 million.

City won only two more Premiership matches in 1993-94 and in July, prolific striker Chris Sutton went to Blackburn for a British record £5 million.

New faces arrived, among them centre-half Jon Newsome from Leeds for a Canary record fee of £1 million, and for the first half of the season, Deehan's team defied the odds and stayed on the fringe of the pack chasing European qualification.

But the departures continued. Strikers Efan Ekoku and Mark Robins both went for £1 million when it was clear City were desperately short of experience up front. When goalkeeper Bryan Gunn was stretchered off at Nottingham Forest in December and the Canaries failed to sign experienced cover, they began a relentless slide down the table.

The occasional spirited performance – a draw at Blackburn and victory over Ipswich – postponed the inevitable for Deehan, but when he finally resigned with only five matches left, caretaker boss Gary Megson was handed a thankless task in trying to save City's Premiership status. One point out of a possible 15 was nothing like enough and down City went.

It was a season which finished bitterly, with red card protests against the chairman and mounted police used at Carrow Road to break up demonstrations. By then, Munich and Milan seemed a million miles away.

City's success under Mike Walker was ultimately self-destructive. The rising profile of the manager made him a target for bigger clubs, and when Walker challenged club chairman Robert Chase to 'open the purse strings' in order to keep top players at Carrow Road, confrontation was inevitable. Everton made no secret of their interest in Walker and, disenchanted by City's failure to offer him an improved contract, he resigned on 7 January to take the job at Goodison Park. This picture was taken three days before Walker resigned, on the morning of his final match in charge, a 2-1 home defeat by Newcastle. Goodison proved something of a nightmare for Walker, who was sacked after nine months in charge with his team bottom of the Premiership.

Despite the shock departure of Walker only 24 hours before their third-round FA Cup-tie at Wycombe Wanderers, City, now under John Deehan, kept their nerve to win the match 2-0 and go into the fourth round. But that was the end of their interest in the competition as Manchester United, eventual winners of the trophy, won 2-0 at Carrow Road. The match was marred by controversy over United's French star Eric Cantona, whose ugly challenges on Jeremy Goss and John Polston were condemned by TV pundit Jimmy Hill. Here Cantona and Polston battle for possession.

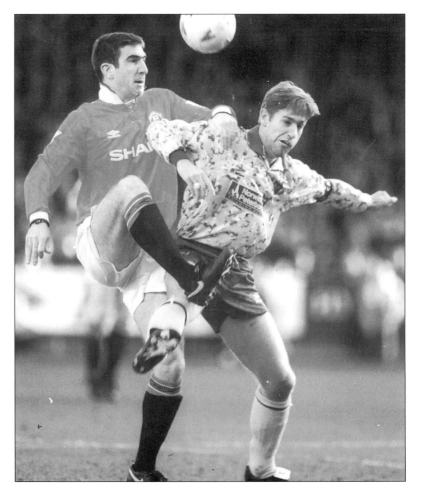

Winger Ruel Fox had become one of the most sought-after stars of the City side, producing his best football during the Walker reign, and he was not long in following his former boss out of the door at Carrow Road. For Fox (left), the FA Cup-tie against Manchester United was his last match for City and three days later he joined Newcastle for £2.25 million, the first of a string of departures which fatally weakened the team's attacking potency.

Just over 10 weeks after resigning as City boss, Mike Walker was back at Carrow Road with his new club, Everton, for a Monday night Premiership fixture. But this was no happy homecoming for him as the Canaries turned on the style to win 3-0 with goals from Ian Culverhouse, Chris Sutton and Mark Bowen. Walker's post-match claim that it was his side playing his way infuriated new boss John Deehan and led to the first public dispute between the two.

City's Premiership results under John Deehan were disappointing in the second half of the 1993-94 season. They drew the first seven League games after Walker's departure, and won only two of their last 19. City also suffered a string of bizarre home defeats, including a 4-3 reverse against Queen's Park Rangers and an even more extraordinary 5-4 defeat by Southampton. Efan Ekoku gets a pat on the back from Ian Crook after one of his two goals against Rangers. Ekoku's days at Carrow Road were numbered, however, and he was sold to Wimbledon for £1 million after a lean start to the next season. He repaid City by scoring the winner against them in both Premiership matches.

City chairman Robert Chase called a Press conference at Carrow Road on 10 July, effectively setting up an auction for the services of striker Chris Sutton. Chase demanded £5 million from prospective buyers by the end of the week, or else Sutton would stay with Norwich. But Blackburn had already made their move, and despite reported interest from Arsenal, the Ewood Park club got their man. The deal brought criticism raining down on the head of the chairman, who had said earlier: "If Chris Sutton is not here at the start of next season, neither will I be." But there he remained, and the big-money sales were not over yet.

Chris Sutton didn't have long to wait for his return to Norwich, Blackburn visiting Carrow Road on 1 October. And Sutton took only four minutes to give his side the lead, here getting the better of Jon Newsome. But Newsome, City's own record buy at £1 million, had the last laugh, scoring a second-half winner as the Canaries hit back to win 2-1. They later took a point from a goalless draw in the return fixture at Blackburn, something of an irony given such a disastrous second half to the season.

Somewhere beneath this pile of bodies is City skipper Jon Newsome after scoring the winner against Blackburn at Carrow Road. Last player to leap on the rest is midfielder Mike Milligan, who made his home debut against Rovers following an £850,000 move from Oldham during the summer. Head in hands is Blackburn skipper Tim Sherwood, another former Canary, who finished the season by lifting the championship trophy.

The biggest single blow suffered by City on their downward spiral towards relegation was the injury sustained by goalkeeper Bryan Gunn in their Premiership match at Nottingham Forest two days after Christmas. A broken and dislocated ankle ruled him out for the rest of the season and well though 19-year-old Andy Marshall performed when thrown in at the deep end, Gunn's command of his area and his defence was undoubtedly missed. The Scottish international goalkeeper was quick to sign a new contract at the end of the season, however, in the hope of helping the Canaries to a quick top-flight return.

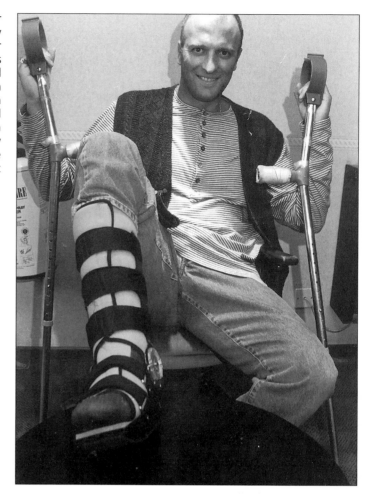

The Mark Robins transfer saga in January 1995 was a public relations disaster for the Canaries. Striker Robins was dropped after the Boxing Day home defeat by Tottenham and, when he said publicly he might be better to seek a move, he found himself completely out of the first-team reckoning. However, two days before the home match against Wimbledon, and the day after City's Coca-Cola Cup quarter-final exit at Bolton, manager John Deehan announced that he had held 'clear the air' talks with Robins and said the striker was back in his squad for the Wimbledon game. The same night, Leicester City offered £1 million for Robins and suddenly he was on his way out of Carrow Road after all. Robins was the fourth striker to depart in less than a year, following Fox, Sutton and Ekoku, for a total of £9.25 million – an increasingly sore point with supporters as City headed for relegation.

Crewe Alexandra striker Ashley Ward was the man brought in by manager John Deehan to try to revitalise the goalscoring department and he made the perfect start, with two goals on his debut against Chelsea at Carrow Road. He followed that with the winner at Crystal Palace, and when he scored against Newcastle on New Year's Eve, Ward had four goals from his first five games. But after the sale of Robins, he lacked an experienced partner for the rest of the season and his final tally of eight goals from 25 Premiership games, though comfortably making him highest scorer for City, seemed to suggest he would have appreciated more robust assistance. Ward here challenges Earl Barrett of Everton in City's 2-1 defeat at Goodison Park.

Southampton's visits to Carrow Road have often provided drama – and just occasionally of the rough and tumble variety. In 1992, the Saints had two players sent off as they lost an FA Cup quarter-final replay at Norwich. Two years later they won a remarkable match 5-4 with a last-minute goal from Ken Monkou. And in 1995, Monkou was in the thick of the action again, here moving in to settle an argument between City skipper Jon Newsome and the Saints' Richard Hall. Newsome and Ashley Ward (left) were both on the scoresheet as City hit back to draw 2-2.

City's world came crumbling down around them when they suffered a humiliating FA Cup fifth-round exit at Everton, beaten 5-0 on the ground where they had won 5-1 less than 18 months earlier. Their fate was effectively sealed by the sending-off of skipper Jon Newsome. Manager John Deehan had opted to play on-loan goalkeeper Simon Tracey, instead of Andy Marshall, whose heroics in the previous round against Coventry had done so much to see City into the last 16. Tracey suffered a nightmare afternoon and never played for the Canaries again.

One man against the crowd – City boss John Deehan tries to get his instructions over to his players during the FA Cup defeat at Goodison Park. Everton were in no mood to relax their grip, however, and their 5-0 win served as a warning to the rest of the nation. Revived by Joe Royle's arrival as manager, they went on to beat Newcastle, Tottenham and Manchester United to lift the trophy at Wembley.

John Deehan described the FA Cup defeat at Everton as 'the lowest point of my managerial career'. Until then, it was. After what he described as 'a period of mourning' City faced successive Premiership games against Manchester United and Blackburn. United won 2-0 at Carrow Road and a similar defeat at Ewood Park might well have ended Deehan's reign, yet the Canaries rallied and might have done better than a goalless draw against the prospective champions. The result at least postponed talk of the sack for Deehan.

A sign of the times – City chairman Robert Chase meets the media. Behind him, a montage of sponsors' logos all but obscures the soccer action going on underneath, a fitting analogy with the game in the 1990s as League sponsors, club sponsors and kit sponsors all demand their share of attention. Chase was announcing a buy-back scheme for club shares with the long-term intention of a stock market flotation, a plan which was postponed when the unthinkable – relegation – became a reality.

With Bryan Gunn out of action and Jeremy Goss sidelined after a hernia operation, the burden fell more and more on City's youngsters to help dig them out of trouble in the Premiership. Andy Marshall, Andy Johnson, Darren Eadie, Robert Ullathorne, Daryl Sutch, Jamie Cureton and Ade Akinbiyi were all thrust into a new situation as the battle for points became desperate. But at first it seemed the Canaries would cope. Visiting West Ham, they led 2-0 with goals from Eadie and Ullathorne, only for the Hammers to snatch a point with two late goals. Here, Eadie (left) is pursued by Sutch as they celebrate the first goal at Upton Park.

City midfielder Andy Johnson was the victim of a bizarre refereeing blunder during the 2-2 draw at West Ham – given the red card in a case of mistaken identity. Substitute referee Martin Sims sent Johnson off after Spencer Prior had committed a second bookable offence. Prior, already convinced of his fate, started to walk to the dressing-room, only for the referee to produce the red card for Johnson, who was sporting a similar crew-cut hairstyle. The decision was later reversed by the FA and defender Prior served a one-match suspension. But the incident hardly helped City's morale as they slid down the table.

Victory over Ipswich Town seemed to have lifted the spectre of relegation from Carrow Road on a Monday night in March. A 3-0 win gave City their first League double over Town for 43 years and brought them back into the top half of the table, albeit briefly. But they had to wait until the controversial sending-off of Ipswich veteran John Wark before getting on top, this goal from Jamie Cureton breaking the deadlock and others from Ashley Ward and Darren Eadie wrapping up victory. Poor Ipswich were already as good as down, but little did City realise that seven straight defeats lay ahead, sentencing them to a place in the Endsleigh League with their Suffolk rivals.

Defeat by Newcastle marked the end of the Walker reign and so it was with John Deehan, who resigned as manager on Sunday, 9 April, the day after a 3-0 defeat at St James' Park, City's third reverse in eight days. By now they were deep in relegation trouble, and Deehan spoke of making the 'ultimate sacrifice' for the good of the club. For such a popular player and successful coach with the Canaries, Deehan's unhappy managerial reign was a sad note on which to end, and his resignation did not prevent his team from taking the plunge out of the Premiership.

First-team coach Gary Megson was handed the unenviable job of trying to save City from the drop with only five matches left. He was told the job would be his permanently if he could steer the Canaries to safety. But Megson had a mountain to climb. He had even had to come out of retirement to play at Leicester in Deehan's penultimate match in charge, because of City's injury and suspension problems. He certainly instilled more fight into the side in the remaining games, but his first match in charge was a 1-0 home defeat by Nottingham Forest and the writing was on the wall after another 1-0 reverse at Tottenham on Easter Monday.

City's last realistic chance of maintaining their survival bid came in their penultimate home match against Liverpool. The Anfield side had already booked a place in Europe by winning the Coca-Cola Cup, and so had little to play for. But they still beat City 2-1 and made relegation a near certainty. Robert Ullathorne's equaliser gave Norwich some hope, but it was a late winner from Ian Rush which sealed their fate. The match was marked by a half-time red card protest against the policies of chairman Robert Chase, and further disturbances outside the stadium after the match.

The Canaries were still clinging grimly to a Premiership lifeline with a one-goal lead in their final away match at Leeds when the match turned on a controversial penalty award. Referee Alan Wilkie gave Leeds the spot-kick ten minutes from time for what he claimed was a foul by Rob Newman on Tony Yeboah, though TV replays seemed to confirm that there was no contact. City's protests were in vain and Gary McAllister stepped up to beat Andy Marshall from the spot.

A 1-1 draw still offered City the faintest mathematical chance of survival, but any thoughts of that were banished in injury-time when, for the second home game in a row, Carlton Palmer conjured up a late winner for Leeds. For City skipper Jon Newsome (left), a Leeds old boy, and Rob Newman, the despair is plain to see. For the Leeds fans behind the goal, trips into Europe next season are on the agenda.

The Canaries' search for a new manager ended on Tuesday, 13 June, with the appointment of Martin O'Neill on a two-year contract. The 43-year-old former Northern Ireland international was recruited after five highly-successful years with Wycombe Wanderers, ending a month of speculation, during which caretaker manager Gary Megson, Barnet manager Ray Clemence and Raith Rovers manager Jimmy Nicholl were all in the frame. Nicholl even toured Carrow Road the day before his former Northern Ireland colleague O'Neill was appointed. On the day of his appointment, O'Neill, a popular choice with the fans, said "the Premiership is the promised land and we have to get back there as quickly as possible."

Home Sweet Home

ICH | NORWICH, SATURDAY, AUGUST 31, 1935

ST. LEGER TRIAL	NORWICH CITY F.C.'s	OSTENDE G
STAKES	NEW GROUND OPENED	PRIX
AT GATWICK		GORDON RIC
		AFTER THE

NORWICH CITY F.C.'s NEW GROUND OPENED

Mr. Colman Performs Ceremony

CITY QUICKLY SCORE IN NEW HOME

ordon Richards Scores On Milldoria

GREEN AND YELLOW BARRIER CUT

Aggressive Start Against West Ham

NTER MIST UPSETS ODDS LAID ON RAMADAN

LOCHHEAD LOSES TOSS BUT OPENS THE NORWICH

The sun broke through the rain clouds at Carrow Road to-day a few moments after

'A monument of local enterprise and achievement' – that's how City's new home ground at Carrow Road was described on the day it opened for the Second Division home match against West Ham United on Saturday, 31 August 1935. Construction of the stadium was completed in 82 days. City won 4-3 with captain Doug Lochhead scoring the first-ever goal at the club's new home. A crowd of 29,779 saw the match. It was two years before the Barclay Stand was built to provide cover for 10,000 fans at the Thorpe End.

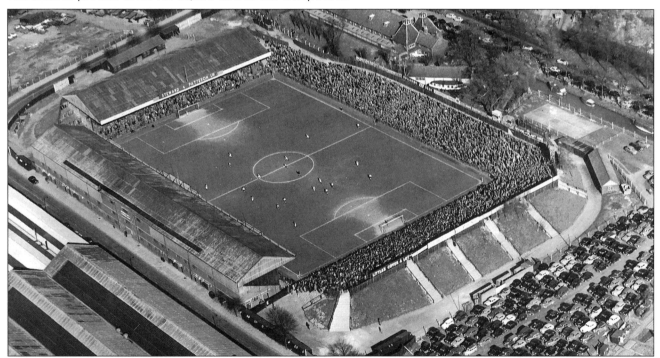

Bright spring sunshine provided perfect conditions for photographer George Swain in April 1955, when this aerial picture of Carrow Road was taken. Only two sides of the ground were under cover at the time, the original Main Stand (nearest the camera) and the Barclay Stand at the Thorpe End of the ground. The South Stand was built in the early 1960s and the River End terrace bulldozed in 1979 to make way for the present two-tier structure. The Main Stand was substantially damaged by fire in 1984 and rebuilt, with its reopening in 1986 as the City Stand. The Barclay terrace was demolished, despite protests from its terrace faithful, in 1992 and replaced by the current £3 million all-seater stand. The day this picture was taken, the Canaries were busy losing 2-1 to Gillingham in a Division Three South fixture. Note the style of cars parked behind the River End goal, and the absence of floodlights. These were installed the following year.

The floodlights at Carrow Road were first switched on in October 1956 at a cost of £9,000, but the board were later criticised by the 1957 Appeal Committee for their extravagance! This picture was taken in 1959, two days before the Canaries' FA Cup quarter-final replay against Sheffield United, for which extra lighting was introduced. Club officials are out in the centre of the pitch to check the effect.

Aerial shot of Carrow Road in the early 1960s, taken from the floodlight pylon in the corner where the Barclay Stand met the newly-covered South Stand. This was when ground capacity was at its peak at Norwich, with the stadium capable of holding well over 40,000. A club record 43,984 attended the FA Cup quarter-final against Leicester in 1963. The original Main Stand (top right) survived until 1984 when it was severely damaged by fire.

When three sides of Carrow Road were still terracing, it was possible to walk around three sides to pick your favourite vantage point. This picture, taken in March 1972, shows the view from the point where the old River End terrace met the South Stand. The corresponding spot is now occupied by the Disabled Stand.

City's return to Division One in 1975 was followed by the decision to increase the amount of seating in Carrow Road. In what proved a controversial move, 5,000 seats were installed on the old South Stand terrace, cutting the capacity of that part of the ground by half. Though the move attracted many new season-ticket holders, bringing in extra finance before the season began, it also alienated many terrace regulars. The colour of the seats – red and blue – was incongruous and today they stand out like a sore thumb in an otherwise colour co-ordinated Carrow Road.

The wreckage left by rioting Manchester United fans at Carrow Road on 2 April 1977, gave ground staff a huge clearing-up job. Some of the debris was used as missiles and hurled at police manning the exits into Carrow Road below. The disturbances were the subject of a special report on the BBC's *Nationwide* programme on the Monday night after the game.

Time to survey the Barclay Stand damage left when Manchester United visited Carrow Road. Repairs had to be swiftly carried out as City faced home matches on the next two Saturdays, the first of them the local derby against Ipswich Town. The scene also illustrates the way clubs were forced to introduce cage work to combat the hooligan problem of the period. The Barclay was split into pens in the early 1970s and more extensive and gruesome fences went up over the decade. Not until the Hillsborough disaster of 1989 was the trend reversed.

City manager Ken Brown stands amid the charred remains of the centre section of the old Main Stand after the Carrow Road fire of 25 October 1984. The boardroom and dressing-rooms took the worst of the blaze, which started at 3am. It posed immediate difficulties for staff at Carrow Road, for City were at home to Queen's Park Rangers two days later. Season-ticket holders were relocated in other parts of the ground and the teams had to use temporary changing facilities. The match went ahead and City won 2-0.

An aerial view of the extent of the damage caused by the Main Stand fire. The blaze came less than a year before the Canaries reached their 50th anniversary at Carrow Road, but they could be grateful that it happened when the ground was empty and nobody was injured. Just seven months later, another wooden stand at Valley Parade, Bradford, caught fire during a match against Lincoln City and 56 supporters died.

This mangled plastic was all that was left in row upon row of what used to be tip-up seats in the Main Stand at Carrow Road after the fire. City fans had to get used to a three-sided stadium for the next season and a half until the new City Stand was in use at the start of the 1986-87 season.

The Milk Cup stands proudly in the charred skeleton of City's Main Stand. Once this section of the ground housed the trophy room. Many souvenirs collected over the years were destroyed in the blaze of 1984, including a bust of former chairman Geoffrey Watling.

It wasn't just managers Bond and Brown who took their sons under their wing in a key role at Carrow Road. Groundsman Russell Allison and son Russell junior worked in harness, keeping the pitch and surrounds in good order. Russell senior retired officially in 1989 and was given a surprise party, but continued to help out at the ground, before his untimely death in 1992. Father and son are pictured in 1986 in the bleak mid-winter, following a postponement.

Virtually the last remnant of the original Carrow Road ground was replaced in the summer of 1993 when the pitch was dug up and relaid, with a new drainage system and undersoil heating installed at the same time. The playing surface was, until then, the very same one laid in 1935, while all around it the ground changed dramatically. To the right of picture was the latest addition, the new £3 million Barclay Stand, opened in 1992.

Bathed in sunshine, the all-seater Carrow Road of 1994, with the Barclay Stand visible to the far right and only the South Stand out of camera. Plans to redevelop the South Stand were on the table in 1995, but were put on hold after City's relegation to the Endsleigh League. The rest of the stadium has all been redeveloped over the past 15 years, with the River End Stand completed in 1980, the City Stand in 1986 and the Barclay Stand in 1992.

Special Guests

King George VI became the first reigning monarch to attend a Second Division match when he visited Carrow Road on Saturday, 29 October 1938, and he met both teams before the Canaries played Millwall. There was little cheer otherwise, however, for City, who lost 2-0 and were relegated at the end of the season. Tom Smalley, City captain, is shown introducing his players to the King, who is reported to have stayed to see only 15 minutes of the match. Perhaps he had an idea of what the outcome would be.

A crowd of 21,593 was at Carrow Road for the King's visit and here he meets the Millwall team who spoiled the party by winning 2-0. Carrow Road had been open for only three years but this was the second biggest attendance of the season as City's poor results led to relegation on goal-average.

Prince Andrew, then aged 12, arrives at Carrow Road with the Bishop of Norwich, the Rt Revd Maurice Wood, to see City's replayed Football League Cup semi-final on Wednesday, 3 January 1973. Chelsea were the visitors.

The Prince's visit coincided with one of the great nights in City's history as they beat Chelsea 1-0 to seal a 3-0 aggregate victory and go on to meet Tottenham at Wembley. Here he talks to club chairman Geoffrey Watling as they take their seats for the match.

One of the Canaries' best-known supporters, Lord Prior is seen on one of his frequent visits to Carrow Road, in January 1981, when he presented a cheque for £206,000 to club chairman Sir Arthur Smith, a grant from the Football Grounds Improvements Trust for safety work carried out. At the time, James Prior was MP for Lowestoft and Employment Secretary.

The Duchess of Kent visited Carrow Road on 14 February 1987, to officially open the City Stand. The Canaries met Manchester City in a 1-1 draw. Here, City players are introduced to the Duchess by skipper Steve Bruce (right). Lining up (left to right) are Tony Spearing, Bryan Gunn, Kenny Brown, Ian Butterworth and Kevin Drinkell.

The Duchess is a more familiar visitor at Wimbledon through her love of tennis, and she enjoyed talking about the game with City manager Ken Brown, whose daughter Amanda was among the top-ranked British women and competed in the Wightman Cup. She also received a basket of flowers from ball-boy Jonathan Munby, watched by City chairman Robert Chase.

John Major, Prime Minister and well-known Chelsea supporter, gets acquainted with an inflatable canary during his visit to Carrow Road on Saturday, 30 March 1991. He didn't prove a lucky charm, however. The Canaries were well beaten, 3-0 by Manchester United. Mr Major inspected some of City's latest facilities, including the purpose-built stand for disabled supporters.

Franz Beckenbauer never graced Carrow Road as a player, but he was there on Wednesday, 3 November 1993, as Bayern Munich provided City's UEFA Cup second-round opponents. The Bundesliga team were held to a 1-1 draw and so went out 3-2 on aggregate. Here, the 'Kaiser' signs for an autograph hunter and meets the media at Norwich Airport.

England managers made frequent visits to Carrow Road after City's arrival in Division One, but Terry Venables' trip to Norwich in February 1995 was more than the average spying mission. He was a special guest of the Canaries as he viewed the club's new £1 million-plus training complex at Colney. Here Venables chats to some of City's young recruits. He went away well impressed and his England predecessor Graham Taylor was one of the next to visit, looking at the possibility of a similar complex for his club, Wolves.

A Matter of Style

Left: Formal studio poses were the fashion in 1906, and City players sat for photographers Albert E.Coe, of London Street, Norwich. The club still wore blue and white halves at this stage, and the shirt worn here by John Byrne seems on close inspection to have seen better days, but the player himself is immaculate. Byrne was a soldier in the Boer War for 15 months, and made four first-team appearances for Norwich at left-half in 1906.

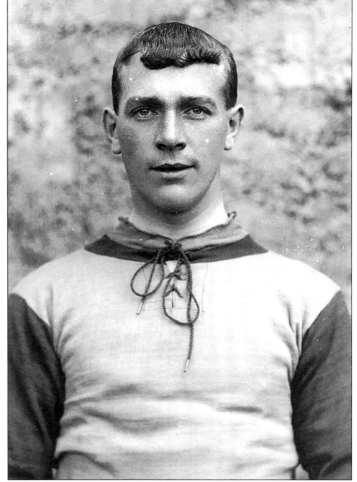

City had switched to yellow and green shirts by the time Fred 'Sonny' Wilkinson made his debut in 1910. Those laced collars were still part of the attire, a feature which has come back into fashion in the 1990s with many clubs. Right-half Wilkinson made 68 first-team appearances for City between 1910 and 1912.

Left: Here's what the best-dressed City footballer was wearing in 1911, looking as proud as a peacock. James Peacock, in fact, an outside-left who played four times for the first team. Born in Peterborough, Peacock also played for Ipswich Town and Norwich CEYMS.

179

City were into yellow and green stripes when this team picture was taken in 1920-21, by which time kit had moved a little more into the 20th century! Open collar shirts, thick socks and hefty shin pads are all visible here, and it was a look which did not change dramatically for the next 40 years. This was City's first season in the Football League, in Division Three.

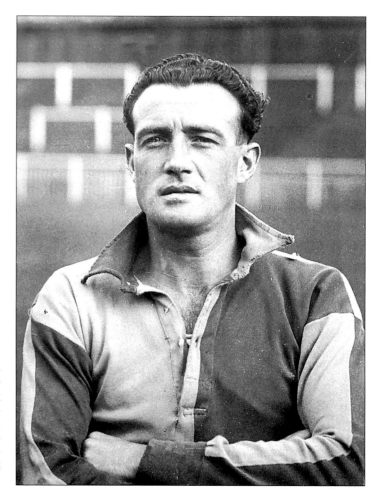

Players of the immediate post-war era often speak of how heavy their kit was, especially in wet weather. One can sympathise when one looks at the shirt worn by Maurice Tobin in this picture from 1946. Definitely not the ideal material for a hot August afternoon.

Those shirts were a little more lightweight by the early 1950s and City turned out in silk that would have graced the sport of kings. Centre-forward Tom Johnston, hero of the FA Cup triumph at Arsenal in 1954, is shown in action at Carrow Road.

By the late 1950s, shorts were beginning to get shorter and shirts a good deal simpler, with the simple V-neck a feature of the City kit at the end of the decade. Ron Ashman presents his 1959 FA Cup semi-finalists – all except Bryan Thurlow – for the camera, and immaculate they look. Goalkeepers were still locked into the dark ages, however, forced to wear those Polar exploration jerseys.

For a decade which produced such spectacular and at times outrageous fashions, the 1960s was a remarkably sober time for soccer kit. City's FA Cup-tie at Chelsea in 1968 gives a good example. Those hoops on City's socks and the white stripe down Chelsea's shorts are the nearest one gets to revolutionary design for these clean-cut lads, goalkeeper Kevin Keelan looking distinctly uncomplicated compared to the goalkeepers of today. However, those 1960s shirts experienced something of a revival among supporters in the 1990s when reissued in replica form. How long before the teams are wearing them again?

Albert Bennett introduced a new fashion to Carrow Road in 1969 as the first City player to wear white boots. The former England Under-23 international, who joined the Canaries from Newcastle, was sporting his white boots before the trend became more popular in the early 1970s. Arsenal stars such as Alan Ball and Frank McLintock were among those to follow suit, and at one stage, players experimented with boots where the studs in the heel were set in a rotating wheel. It was thought the innovation would reduce ankle injuries.

The '70s saw the start of a revolution in soccer kit as a string of top clubs followed the lead of the England national team in signing up with kit manufacturers Admiral. City donned Admiral strip in 1976 and wore it for five seasons, with the company emblem woven into strips on the sleeves and shorts. The design was distinctly sober, however, compared to what was to follow in the 1980s and 1990s. England's poor performances under Don Revie led one cartoonist to portray the manager with 'Little Midshipman' emblazoned on his track suit. Kevin Reeves is pictured in the City strip in 1979.

City changed strips more often than they changed divisions in the 1980s and they introduced their sixth different shirt of the decade in 1989 when they signed a sponsorship deal with Japanese sports shoe manufacturers Asics, who not only became kit sponsors but main club sponsors, too. Dale Gordon (left) is pictured in the Asics strip, up against Mike Hazard of Swindon.

The Canaries' new shirt design in 1992 was the most unorthodox yet, as manufacturers Ribero came up with a strip more akin to beachwear. It was described by one commentator as 'scrambled egg and cress' but quickly became popular, not least by association with a winning team as City took the new Premier League by storm. Mark Bowen here shows what the latest table-toppers are wearing.

One wonders how City goalkeepers such as Charlie Dennington or Ken Nethercott would have reacted if handed a jersey such as this on match days. But the transformation in kit design has probably had more dramatic effect on goalkeepers' attire than any other player. Bryan Gunn dons the latest design at the start of the 1994-95 season.

Baggy shorts are back in vogue in the 1990s and City were no exception when they introduced another new strip in 1994, produced by Mitre, and reverting to a less complicated look. Mark Robins does the honours for the photo-call.

A neat contrast in designs as City parade their new change strip in a pre-season friendly against Belgian side KV Mechelen in August 1994. The Canaries' plaid creation worn by Jeremy Goss, looks relatively modest when compared to their opponents' kit.

The Old Boy Network

Cornishman Percy Varco, City's prolific centre-forward of the late 1920s, was back in Norwich in 1972 for the launch of Ted Bell's book, *On the Ball, City*, A fish merchant and also Mayor of Fowey in the years after his retirement from soccer in 1933, Varco died in Fowey in 1982, aged 77.

At home in Norwich, Bernard Robinson, City wing-half of the 1930s and 1940s and one of the best servants in club history, with one of his scrapbooks from his playing days. But for the war years, he would surely have passed the 500 mark in appearances by some distance.

Three of City's best-known faces from the 1950s met up again at a players' reunion at the Duke of Norfolk pub in Norwich. Pictured (left to right) are Bill Lewis, the left-back who made 256 senior appearances for the Canaries; Johnny Gavin, leading goalscorer in club history with 132 goals; and Ron Hansell, who was with City for seven years as an inside-right and went on to be a Yarmouth Town player and coach.

Four of City's FA Cup heroes of 1959 were reunited 25 years later when Errol Crossan (second left) made his first return to England since going back to his native Canada at the end of his playing career. A players' reunion was staged to coincide with his visit at the Kingsway public house, close to Carrow Road. There to greet Crossan were (left to right) Ken Nethercott, Sandy Kennon and Bryan Thurlow.

Above: Ron Ashman and Alf Kirchen came from two different eras in club history. One spent 22 years with City as player and manager. The other was sold to Arsenal for £6,000 when his City career was barely off the ground, but returned as a director at Carrow Road in the 1950s. The two met up again in the summer of 1994 as former Canaries gathered for a book and video launch.

Right: Duncan Forbes celebrated 25 years at Carrow Road in September 1993, and was out on the pitch just to test if the old ball balancing act was still up to scratch. Forbes, by this time City's chief scout, also turned back the clock by modelling the relaunched 1960s-style City kit, a popular nostalgia kick for long-serving fans.

Three of City's finest all-time players – and teammates from the early 1960s – were among those reunited at Carrow Road in July 1994 for a book and video launch, (left to right) Roy McCrohan, Ollie Burton and Terry Allcock. Burton, a Welsh international half-back, was a member of City's League Cup-winning team in 1962 and, after moving to Newcastle for £30,000 in 1963, helped them to Fairs Cup glory six years later.

Fans for All Seasons

The Canary cavalcade swept into Sheffield for the FA Cup quarter-final at Bramall Lane on 28 February 1959, complete with all manner of home-made hats, placards and trophies and equipped with plenty of food and drink for the long day trip north. They were not disappointed. City earned a replay with a 1-1 draw.

They were up bright and early on Monday, 9 March 1959 – queuing for tickets for City's FA Cup semi-final against Luton the following Saturday. Ted Bell wrote in *On the Ball, City* that Norfolk and beyond was 'in the grip of soccer fever'. After City's initial success over Manchester United, Carrow Road was under almost constant siege. 'Hire purchase debts soared as supporters scraped together the pennies to make the trips to White Hart Lane, Sheffield and Birmingham.'

There must have been a knitwear boom in Norwich and the surrounding towns and villages during the 1959 FA Cup run. How many fans passed their time in the ticket queues, like these two ladies, with the rapid click-click of the knitting needles? No doubt it was well worth the wait to see such an historic chapter in club history unfold.

City's elaborately dressed 'mascots' became part of the FA Cup scene in 1959 as they followed their team's attempt to reach Wembley. Only at Bramall Lane, Sheffield, were they refused permission to parade on the touch-line. It is hard to imagine such a group being permitted on the track in this day and age. The coffin being carried by one fan in this group – at White Hart Lane before the semi-final against Luton – bears the names of City's previous victims in the competition. Luton were not, however, about to join them.

St Andrew's, Birmingham, marked the end of the road for the Canaries in the FA Cup and the end of a marvellous adventure for thousands of supporters. But they were still in good spirits before the semi-final replay against Luton Town. One fan (right) even has a bell, while one of the young ladies at the front of the terrace has the names of the City players stitched into her scarf.

The Barclay Stand at Carrow Road packed for the Division Two local derby against Ipswich Town on 3 February 1968. It was another four years before the Barclay was to be split into separate pens, after which a whole variety of fences went up during the 1970s in an attempt to keep rival fans apart and cut out crowd trouble. The terrace, so beloved of its regulars, was demolished in 1992 to make way for the new £3 million double-decker stand.

Where better to be in the Swinging Sixties than Chelsea? City fans of all ages mingle happily on the terraces at Stamford Bridge on 17 February 1968, before the Canaries' FA Cup fourth-round tie. They were beaten 1-0 in front of a crowd of 57,987, but the defeat was no disgrace against the previous season's beaten Finalists.

The River End terrace, packed during the 1971-72 promotion campaign. It was a time when the youngest and smallest were still fed through to the front of the terrace to get a better view of proceedings. Note the scaffolding at the back for the benefit of Anglia TV cameras. *Match of the Week* covered City's games from behind the goal until 1972, when the cameras moved to the spot they still occupy, on the gantry below the roof of the South Stand.

This fan wants to tell the whole world that City are champions of the Second Division. He produced his own loud hailer for the trip to Watford at the end of the 1971-72 season. The rattle is something of a throwback to a bygone era.

Arguments over which team merited the title 'Pride of Anglia' have raged for years, but these City fans had no doubt as they paraded the flag before the final match of the 1971-72 season at Watford. The Canaries were already promoted and a 1-1 draw at Vicarage Road gave them the Second Division championship.

A pitch invasion of the innocuous kind, unlike those which many clubs were to experience in the troubled 1970s. This time, however, it is simply the Canaries' followers celebrating the Second Division championship at Vicarage Road, Watford, in 1972.

The style of trousers and footwear and the hint of Bay City Rollers tartan make this unmistakably 1975. The date is 26 April and the scene is Fratton Park, where thousands of City fans gathered for a promotion celebration. The Canaries beat Portsmouth 3-0 to book the third promotion place and return to Division One at the first attempt. Their only rivals for third place, Sunderland, were beaten at Aston Villa the same day, a defeat which ended their chance of going up.

These two gentlemen became City's best-known fans through the cartoons of Edgar Henry Banger. 'Canary and Dumpling', instantly recognisable symbols of the city of Norwich and the county of Norfolk, figured in the pages of the *EDP's* sister football paper, the *Pink 'Un*, for many years. The artist died in March 1968, but as a tribute to him the Canary and Dumpling were reintroduced in 1980 as mascots for the team. The identity of those beneath the costumes remained, however, a closely guarded secret.

An estimated 10,000 City fans made their way to Hillsborough, Sheffield, on 15 May 1982, for what proved to be a joyful promotion celebration. The Canaries were beaten 2-1 by Sheffield Wednesday in the final match of the Division Two campaign, but Leicester – the only team who could have pipped them for third place – managed only a 0-0 draw with Shrewsbury, so the defeat didn't matter. The banner 'Going Up' in the middle of the picture was justified.

Fancy dress was the order of the day for some City fans when they travelled to Villa Park for the FA Cup semi-final against Everton in 1989. The Pink Panther mingled happily with the inflatable canaries, but deflation awaited them all as Everton won 1-0.

Sometimes, defeat is just too much to bear. There were only tears for souvenirs for these two young City fans after their team's FA Cup semi-final defeat by Sunderland at Hillsborough in April, 1992. The Canaries went into the match firm favourites against struggling Second Division opponents, but lost 1-0, their second semi-final defeat in four seasons. Some 18,000 Norwich fans went home bewildered by the performance.

City fans were made to feel very much part of the scene when their side visited Oldham in November 1992. The most loyal members of Club Canary, the travel organisation set up by City in 1981, were offered a return flight to the match at the cost of a normal coach return, as reward for their support and in recognition of an inconvenient kick-off time with the match switched to a Monday night for Sky TV. The City team then flew back with the fans, giving them the perfect chance to congratulate Mark Robins on his hat-trick in a 3-2 win – and pose at Norwich Airport with their hero.

Thousands turned out at Carrow Road on a summer evening in August 1993 when there wasn't even a game to watch – in good voice and bedecked in yellow and green. The reason? City fans were chosen to take part in filming the title sequence for BBC Television's *Match Of The Day* programme, passing a giant flag over their heads bearing the name of the show.

City achieved nationwide acclaim to a degree they had not known since 1959 when they made their first European venture in 1993, and the supporters revelled in the new experience of travelling to Arnhem, Munich and Milan to see the team in action. These fans were in buoyant mood outside the San Siro Stadium – rechristened the Giuseppe Meazza Stadium – before the second leg of their third-round tie against Internazionale.

Banners from Diss, Sheringham, Thetford and Thorpe were among those on show as City fans proudly took the chance to display a little slice of Norfolk in the massive, space age stadium in Milan. And in spite of the Canaries' 1-0 defeat, they stayed long after the final whistle to cheer Mike Walker and his players.

Subscribers

R E Abbott
W Allen
Ross Allison
Mr Peter James Allum
Tim Amphlett
David Andrew
Frank Annison
Mr & Mrs D H Argent
Guy Ayers
Robert W Bainbridge
Ann Baker
Kevin R Baldwin
Chris Bamber
J H Banyard
H & D Barnes
Henry William John Barrett
Karen L Basham
Roger Clive Bean
Ian Robert Beckett
Luke Bell
Chris Betts
Mrs Ellen Betts
Les Berwick
Terry Bilverstone
Richard Bland
Mr & Mrs A H Blyth
Robert Bone
Richard Andrew Brady
Jonathan Brighton
David Britcher
Stephen Britcher
Richard Brooks
Terence Brotherhood
Ian Brown
Mark Brown
Michael A Brown
Mr Stuart Brown
Simon Browne
Jeremy Burton
Michael Burton
J Butcher
Julian Canham
David C Cannell
Mr Paul Carter
Amanda Chapman
Brian A Chapman
Carol Clark
John Clarke
Paul Clynch
Daphne Collins

B P &H Colman
Ernie Colman
Richard Cook
Andrew Cooke
Dale Cooper
Mr Stuart Coppen
John Corcoran
Neil W Cousins
Peter F Cresswell
Mr A Crick
Mr P Crick
Adrian D Crotch
David Crown
Mr Geoffrey T Cuffley
Mr Peter R Cuffley
Hayley Cunningham
M R Cunningham
Jonathan Mark Dack
David Davenport
Peter Davey
Pauline Dawson
Jim Distill
Mr Kevin Doran
Peter & Andreas Dornonville de la
    Cour (Aabyhoj, Denmark)
David Dowe
Kevin Dowe
Mr Perry Dyball
James & Eliot Eagle
M R Eagle
Mr J Easey
Tim East
Brian John Elgar
M H Elias
R G Elias
V H Elias
Neil Elsegood
Mrs Juliette Elwick
Chris Ellwood
Craig Farr
Roger Farrow
Mr S Farrow
T E Fenn
Janet Ann Finnshore & John M
    Arnup
A G Firrell
Robert Flack
Caroline Isobel Fleet
George Florey
Suzanne Footer

Andrew Fox
Mr Frank Fuller
R H Garman
Dale Gedge
Ronald E Gent
K George
Daren Gilbert
Kevan Gilbert
Trevor Godbold
Andrew Graver
Mr Nick Gray
R W G Green
Ron Grey
Christopher Halls
Martin Hanner
Miss Dorcas A Harboard
Michael James Hardingham
Philip Hardy
Paul Hargest
George William Harmer
Brian Ivan Harold
Gavin Scott Harold
Mr Alan Harper
Kevin Hayes
Gary D Haynes
Austin Hendy
Christopher Herrieven
Dennis J Hicks
Paul Hicks
Chris Higgins, Trafford Arms
Daniel P Hines
Mr Glen Hipperson
Gerald E Hogg
Julian Hogg
Adrian Holman
Kenneth John Holman
Chris Hooker
Andrew Howell
Ivan Roy Howman
Kenneth Malcolm Hubbard
Clive Hudson
Daryl Hurley
Mr Andrew D Jaggard
Joanna Jenney
Mr C Johnson
Stephen Jones
Graeme J Keeler
S P Kempson
Stephen Kennedy
Susan Kennedy

Tony King
Philip David Lagden
Mr David Lathangue
Richard Robert Laxen
David John Lee
Peter Frank Lee
James Leech
W A Lewis
Mr Paul Lindsell
Michael G Ling
Ashley Locke
Jack Loveday
Frederick K Lumley
R A McEwen
Gordon Maggs
Valerie Main
Mrs Sam Mann
Andrew March
Philip Markham
Mel Marrison
Alan Martin
Christopher Martins
Roger Martins
Jason A C Masala
Peter Mendham
William Raymond Mendham
Andrew Menin
Revd Don P Mentch
Lyn Mepham
Colin S Mickleburgh JP
Diane E Miller
William Edward Miller
Robert Martin Mitchell
Mr James Moore
Mr Robert Moore
Vaughan William Moore
C J Morton
Jonathan Moule
Arthur Moy
Mike Munroe
Laura Murphy
Paul Murrell
Philip John Neale
Mr Cameron Newark
John Norfolk
Stuart Oakey
Mrs A Osborne
Daniel Overy
Mr & Mrs T R Page

V C Page
Mr A P Palmer
E J Parmenter
G Pask
John D Patrick
David Pease
Anthony Peek
Philip C Peeling
Ian D Phillpot
Mark A Piggott
Martin Pilkington
John Plane
Kevin J Playford
Mrs Heather Plume
Stephen Pole
Derek Pratt
C A Pyle
E H Read
Darrell Reed
Kevin Reynor
David J Richards
Mr Kenneth Richardson
Scott Richmond
Shane Richmond
Shane Risby
Emma Roache
Sophie Roberts
Christopher Rose
Timothy M Ross
Murray C Rout
Mr Trevor J Rust
Karl & Simon Rutterford
Daniel & Peter Rye
Alan Schmincke
Richard & James Scott
Ryan Michael Seed
A E Sexton
Ian Shimmen
Eric Shingles
James Singleterry
Kelvin Sloper & Kay Barwick
Alan John Smith
Mr Brian David Smith
Mr Roger Smith
Mr S R Smith
Tony Smith
Tony Smith
Richard Soloman
Mr D R Spendloff

Mr R R Spendloff
Alan Stannard
Alex Sutton
D J Taylor
John R G Taylor
Mr Christopher Thompson
Geraldine M Thompson
David Thornhill
Jane & Mark Thorpe
Steve Tillett
Ms S Timm
Les Trimble
Stephen Tuck
Andrew Turner
David James Turner
Emily Ruth Turner
Alan Utting
Christopher Utting
Darren Utting
Terence W Varley & Rachel
    Stevens
Mr Richard Vincent
Mr J Waller
A Ward
Adrian Ward
Adrian S Watling
Geoffrey Watling
Geoffrey Watling
Geoffrey Watling
Rodney Watson
Helen Watts
N J Webb
Paul Webb
Derek Wells
Ted Wells
Richard Whitbourn
Edward Wiles
Andrew Wilkinson
S M Willgoss
Leslie Williams
Keith Williamson
Mr Jeremy Wilson
Jack Wiseman
Barry Woodrow
James Woodrow
Ruth & Alf Wooltorton
Simon Worley
David Yarberry